D1591148

John Henry Newman
A Bibliographical Catalogue
of His Writings

John Henry Newman

A Bibliographical Catalogue
of His Writings

Vincent Ferrer Blehl, S.J.

Published for the Bibliographical Society
of the University of Virginia
by the University Press of Virginia
Charlottesville

THE UNIVERSITY PRESS OF VIRGINIA
Copyright © 1978 by the Rector and Visitors
of the University of Virginia

First published 1978

Frontispiece courtesy of The Oratory,
Birmingham, England

Library of Congress Cataloging in Publication Data
Blehl, Vincent Ferrer.
John Henry Newman: a bibliographical catalogue of his writings.
Includes index.
1. Newman, John Henry, Cardinal, 1801-1890—Bibliography. I. Virginia. University. Bibliographical Society.
Z8622.B58   [BX4705.N5]   016.262135   77-12141   ISBN 0-8139-0738-1

Printed in the United States of America

To
My Brothers and Sisters
Mrs. Susanne Wahl
Mr. Kendon Stubbs

Sine amicitia vitam esse nullam

Contents

Preface

The present work was begun many years ago in the hope of providing an absolutely complete list not only of all of the writings of John Henry Newman but of all the editions and reprints published during his lifetime, exclusive of translations into foreign languages. The published bibliographies of Newman are both incomplete and, at times, inaccurate. I did not realize, however, how difficult it would be to find a copy of each edition and reprint nor the complicated problems that would demand hour upon hour of research to resolve them. Such, for example, were those connected with *Historical sketches* and *Certain difficulties felt by Anglicans*. Only Newman's correspondence with his publishers made clear how of a two-volume edition of the latter, for example, one was published by one firm and the second by another and how the contents were changed, or again why the order of publication of *Historical sketches*, indicated by asterisks on the spine, did not correspond to the volume numbers which appeared on new title pages substituted for the old ones. These complications are explained in notes to these works.

The correspondence also certified that both Pickering and Burns and Oates would reissue a single volume of a two- or three-volume work as it went out of print, so that the lack of a volume in a certain year does not necessarily indicate that it could not be found but that it may never have been issued in that year. The original goal of providing full information on all editions and reprints was, unfortunately, not to be realized. That James Duffy of Dublin put out the third edition of *Loss and gain* is certain, but since I could not secure a copy of it, I have relied upon John William Cronin's entry in his *Bibliography of John Henry Cardinal Newman* (Washington, D.C.). This is indicated by [C] after the entry. Cronin also lists an edition put out by Burns, London, in the same year, which I have not been able to verify, but, nevertheless, I have listed it as given by Cronin. So also, I was unable to find a copy of the third edition of *Lectures on the present position of Catholics in England* put out by Duffy in 1857, though a copy is listed without full bibliographical detail in *A list of works written and edited by His Eminence Cardinal Newman, in the library of Sir William H. Cope, Bart., at Bramshill* (Portsmouth, 1885). The pirated edition of the *Arians* I have been unable to trace.

Omissions in other cases are relatively unimportant. *The dream of Gerontius*, for example, went through twenty-seven printings by 1890. Stereoplates had been made of it from the beginning, and it was reset, as far as can be ascertained, only once, in 1886, when the old plates were discarded. Again, in the case of some works to which Newman contributed, e.g., a preface, listed in Section C, I have been unable to secure every subsequent reprint and have occasionally relied on secondary sources for information about such reprints. Papers at the Oratory Archives, Birmingham, England, which are published only in part, e.g., an introduction to a paper on scripture which I included under the title "Galileo, scripture, and the educated mind," in the *Essential Newman* (Mentor-Omega Book, New York: The New American Library, 1963), are omitted because the complete papers will eventually be published by the Oratory. Again, I have made no attempt to list Newman's letters to newspapers and periodicals, unless subsequently published separately or in a later work, since all his letters are being included in the *Letters and diaries*. I have likewise omitted works listed in Newman bibliographies which are not strictly speaking works he published or approved for publication, e.g., *The enduement of the Holy Spirit . . .* by a Churchman and by Cardinal Newman, or Pugin's *Church and state . . . ,* third edition, together with letters from Dr. Newman. In the later case a photographic reproduction of a Newman letter was simply bound into the book and does not constitute part of the text.

The information given in each entry is first that which is supplied on the title page of each work. Newman's publishers did not distinguish between editions and impressions in the modern sense of the words, i.e., works reset in type or merely reprinted from original type or stereoplates. Even when a work was stereoplated and reprinted from plates, the word "edition" sometimes appears on the title page. Since no library or collection contains all the editions and impressions of any given work, I could not examine all copies to determine accurately what was an edition and what was an impression. Indeed, one of the purposes of this bibliographical catalogue is to prepare the way for critical editions of Newman's works in which such distinctions will be made. Nevertheless, I have attempted, in some instances, to indicate on the basis of the correspondence a new edition or impression.

When Newman's name does not appear on the title page, I have placed [Anon.] after the title unless his initials occur at the end of the preface, advertisement (i.e., introduction), dedication, postscript, or book. These initials have been placed in square brackets. Where I have supplied a date of publication, it is based upon the correspondence. I have also noted the existence of copies corrected or revised by Newman and held at the Oratory. These corrections, made in pencil or ink, were generally incorporated in the next reprint, but I have indicated when they were not so incorporated. In giving in parentheses the total unnumbered pages of a text, I have not counted title pages and blank pages. These unnumbered pages noted in parentheses usually have a table of contents, a dedication, a title of the first section, or a list of errata. Also, in noting a subsequent reprint, I have sometimes loosely used the phrase "later published as" or "later published in" with reference to a work printed for private circulation. Such works, e.g., *My campaign in Ireland*, are often listed in Newman bibliographies and are generally treated as published writings. Because of the confusion attending the identification of the original volumes of *Historical sketches*, I thought it best in making cross-references to them to indicate only the volume number as given on the substituted title pages.

It may seem strange that two entries are listed as having the same numbered edition on the title page but with a different year and publisher, e.g., *Discussions and arguments on various subjects*, fourth edition, Pickering and Co., 1882, and fourth edition, Longmans, Green and Co., 1888. This occurs as well for the *Arians*, fifth edition; *Discourses addressed to mixed congregations*, seventh edition; *An essay in aid of a grammar of assent*, fifth edition; *Essays critical and historical*, fifth edition; *Idea of a university*, fifth edition; *Sermons preached on various occasions*, sixth edition; *Two essays on biblical and on ecclesiastical miracles*, fifth edition. The explanation is most probably as follows. Starting in 1885 Newman transferred from Pickering and Burns and Oates to Longmans, Green, and Co. the existing stock of some of his works. Presumably Longmans added a new title page but kept the same notation of the edition, since the works were not reprinted at that time.

Subscribing to Emerson's dictum that "a foolish consistency is the hobgoblin of little minds," I have had no hesitancy in arranging the entries in the four parts in different ways, as explained in the notes at the beginning of each part. The general principle of arrangement is primarily alphabetical, as befits a catalogue, and secondarily chronological.

The largest collections of Newman's works in England are at the Oratory, Birmingham; The British Museum; The John Rylands Library, Manchester; and the library of the Jesuits at 31 Farm Street, London. In the United States, there are extensive collections at Regis College, Weston, Mass.; Holy Cross College, Worcester, Mass.; the Boston Athenaeum, the Newman Preparatory School, and the Boston Public Library, Boston, Mass.; the Newberry Library, Chicago; the University of Illinois, Urbana; and Harvard University, Cambridge, Mass. Lastly, there is a collection at the Library of University College, Dublin.

I would like to express my thanks to the American Philosophical Society, Philadelphia, and the Research Council of Fordham University for grants to complete the work, as well as to Mrs. Mary Riley, Research Librarian of Fordham University; Mairead Dennigan Browne, former Librarian of University College, Dublin; Francis Canavan, S.J., who helped locate a number of editions; and to Mark Caldwell, a colleague in the English Department, who assisted me in the research on Newman's publishers. The late Charles Stephen Dessain, of the Oratory, kindly granted permission for the use and quotation of letters in the Archives. Finally, I must thank Joseph E. O'Neill, S.J., for his editorial advice, Frederick J. Dillemuth, S.J., for his encouraging support, and Miss Jane Coyle for her infinite patience in typing the manuscript. Errors and omissions may perhaps be inevitable in a work so detailed as this. I can only plead that I tried to be both accurate and complete, but like many a human effort, it may turn out to be flawed. I should also add that I hope this work will be an aid to Newman scholars and even possibly to one who in the future may undertake to perfect what I have begun.

VINCENT FERRER BLEHL, S.J.

Fordham University

Abbreviations

Apo.	*Apologia pro vita sua.*
Campaign	*My campaign in Ireland. Part I* (printed for private circulation only by A. King & Co. printers to the University of Aberdeen, 1896).
Cope	*List of works written and edited by Cardinal Newman in the library of Sir W. H. Cope Bart.* (Portsmouth: privately printed, 1885).
[C]	John William Cronin, *Bibliography of John Henry Cardinal Newman.* Part I. Books (Washington, D.C.).
D.A.	*Discussions and arguments on various subjects.*
Dev.	*An essay on the development of Christian doctrine.*
Certain diff. *, **	*Certain difficulties felt by Anglicans in Catholic teaching,* 2 vols. published separately: the first (*) by Burns, Oates, & Co., 1876, and the second (**) by Basil Montagu Pickering, 1876.
Certain diff., I, II	*Certain difficulties felt by Anglicans in Catholic teaching,* 2 vols. (1879 and thereafter).
E.C.P.	*Essays on controversial points variously illustrated.*
Ess., I, II	*Essays critical and historical,* 2 vols.
H.S., I, II, III	*Historical sketches,* 3 vols.
Idea	*Idea of a university defined and illustrated.*
Letters and diaries	*The letters and diaries of John Henry Newman,* ed. C. Stephen Dessain et al. (vols. XI to XXII, London: Nelson, 1961–72; vols. XXIII to XXXI, Oxford: Clarendon, 1973–77).
L.U.S.	*Lectures and essays on university subjects.*

Mir.	*Two essays on biblical and on ecclesiastical miracles.*
Moz., I, II	*Letters and correspondence of John Henry Newman*, ed. Anne Mozley, 2 vols. London: Longmans, Green, & Co., 1890.
MP	*Memorials of the past.*
Noel	Elizabeth Ann Noel, "An edition of poems by John Henry Newman" (thesis, University of Illinois, 1956, no. 19,856).
O.S.	*Sermons preached on various occasions.*
O.W.	*Office and work of universities.*
P.S.	*Parochial sermons.*
P.P.S.	*Parochial and plain sermons.*
Prepos.	*Lectures on the present position of Catholics in England.*
S.E.	*Stray essays on controversial points.*
T.T.	*Tracts theological and ecclesiastical.*
V.M., I, II	*Via media*, 2 vols.
VRS	*Verses on religious subjects.*
V.V.	*Verses on various occasions.*
Ward, I, II	Wilfrid Ward, *The life of John Henry Cardinal Newman*, 2 vols. (London, 1912).
[Anon.]	Newman's name not on title page
B.O.	Oratory Archives, Birmingham, England
J.H.N.	John Henry Newman
N	John Henry Newman

Introduction

Newman engaged five major publishers for his works: Rivingtons, Burns, Duffy, Pickering, and Longmans, whose names vary over the years with the acquisition and loss of partners. The following account is based upon the extant correspondence, which is not always complete. It does not attempt, therefore, a definitive narrative but is confined to an overview and, because of the complexity of the material, deals with each publisher separately.

Rivingtons

The firm was started by Charles Rivington (1688-1742), who took over the premises and trade of Richard Chiswell upon the latter's death in 1711. He soon became the leading theological publisher in England. His son John (1720-1792) inherited the business on his father's death and became in 1760 the publisher to the Society for Promoting Christian Knowledge. Upon his death in 1792 the firm was carried on by his two sons, Francis (1745-1822) and Charles (1754-1831). The former's eldest son, John (1779-1841), was admitted into the firm in 1810 and the latter's son, Francis (1805-1885), succeeded to the firm upon the death of Charles in 1831. Francis retired in 1859 and his cousin John continued in partnership with Francis's elder son.[1]

Francis was the publisher of Newman's first book, *The Arians*, which he thought dull,[2] and, if one can judge by a letter written many years later, Newman subsequently was not too happy about the arrangements, for he says " 'publishing at his [Longman's] cost and dividing the profits' are no terms at all—Rivington did

[1]*Dictionary of national biography.*
[2]Letter of N to R. H. Froude, Sept. 13, 1832, *Moz.* I, 242.

that for me with the very first book I published—and accordingly I got £80 perhaps at the end of 10 years."[3] Newman was paid £100 a year by Rivington for editing the *British Critic*, 1838-41, "nothing (I think) for my articles, and nothing to various contributors—I forget details, but I believe it never paid Rivington, or hardly." In another letter he listed figures on some other works, the first two of which were published by Rivingtons.

1. I got £80 for 280 octavo pages of the translation of St. Athanasius, in which I had to translate, transcribe, and put notes, besides various dissertations.
2. I got £50 for my Essay on Ecclesiastical Miracles, which I had to compose, transcribe, and put notes to—pp. 216 octavo.
3. I think I got £27 for my Essay on Miracles in the Encyclopaedia Metrop [olitana]. 60 pages large duodecimo, composed, transcribed and notes.[4]

Upon becoming a Catholic in 1845, Newman surrendered the entire copyright of the *Lyra apostolica*, including his own poems, to John Keble. He considered the copyright of the Tracts for the Times written by Pusey, Keble and Isaac Williams to be their own and claimed only the remainder of the existing edition which he had printed at his own expense. The stock of tracts Newman estimated at the value of £900. He insisted that the copyright of his volume of the *Plain sermons* (vol. 5) in the series *Plain sermons, by contributors to the "Tracts for the Times"* was his and that he had the right to make alterations in the text, if he thought it necessary, and to print the volume himself among his other sermons. Nevertheless, he allowed to Isaac Williams, the editor, the unrestricted use of it.[5]

On January 15, 1853, Francis Rivington sent Newman a list of the number of copies of his works that he had in stock. In reply Newman asked if he could buy them from Rivington and also if he could buy back the copyright of his *Essay on ecclesiastical miracles*, which he had sold to Rivington. The latter agreed to sell them for £400 with the exception of *Plain sermons by con-*

[3]*Letters and diaries*, XIII, 194.
[4]Ibid., XIII, 318, and XVIII, 485.
[5]Ibid., XIII, 193, 202, 227-29, 248, 262, 293, and XV, 332.

tributors to the "Tracts for the Times," vol. 5, which, he said, could not be separated from the series. He also agreed to sell back the copyright on *Miracles* for the original price.[6] Nevertheless, the copyright, at least according to a memorandum of Newman, does not seem to have been transferred until later. "I sent to Mr John Rivington on May 2, 1869 a letter of Mr F. Rivington's of the date of March [?] 1857 in which he, on his own part and Mr Parker's of Oxford gave me the copyright of my Essay on Ecclesiastical Miracles in return for my letting the Rivingtons print small editions of Parochial Sermons volumes 2 and 5. In the same letter Mr F. Rivington declined to take a new edition of my Church of the Fathers."[7]

Accordingly, in the spring of 1853 Newman transferred the copyrights of his Anglican works to William Froude, who, being non-Catholic, would presumably have a better chance of selling them. They were six volumes of *Parochial sermons,* Oxford University *Sermons, Sermons on subjects of the day*, the fifth volume of *Plain sermons, Lectures on justification*, and the *Church of the Fathers, The Arians* being out of print and existing only in a pirated edition. The number of copies in stock Newman listed in a letter to Froude, March 11, 1853.[8] Froude attempted to sell the existing stock to Henry George Bohn, of York Street, Covent Garden, but in this he was unsuccessful, and the stock remained with Rivington.[9] On April 3, 1854, Froude sent to Newman "a Bankpost bill for £30 which I have received from Lumley on account, for the copyright of the Arians. . . . The remainder of the money will be paid as soon as the work is ready to be issued or is issued—or at all events very shortly afterwards."[10] This was the only work that Froude was able to get reprinted. It appeared in 1854, reprinted from the first edition and without any literary corrections such as Newman would have liked to have made.

[6]Ibid., XV, 270 and n. 2.

[7]Ibid., XXIV, 243, n. 1.

[8]Ibid., XV, 331.

[9]Ibid., XV, 331, n. 1.

[10]Ibid., XVI, 101-2.

Meanwhile Rivington had sent a number of copies of the Tracts for the Times to Newman, including some of Pusey's tracts. The latter Newman put at Pusey's disposal.[11] In return Pusey gave Newman leave to reprint, if he wished, Newman's volumes of St. Athanasius in the Library of the Fathers.[12] Years passed without much correspondence between Newman and the firm. There is an extant letter of Rivington to W. J. Copeland, Newman's former curate at Littlemore, February 24, 1864, in which the firm declined to republish the *Parochial sermons*, entire or in selection, for the alleged reason that the number of purchases would be small.[13] After the success of the *Apologia* in 1864, Newman tried again, but they again declined a new edition.[14]

Probably stirred by a remark in the course of controversy in the correspondence columns of the *Guardian*,[15] Newman, on January 25, 1867, asked Copeland if he would allow him to republish his *Parochial sermons* and *Plain sermons* under Copeland's editorship with only literary corrections. The same day, he wrote to William Froude about his plans since Froude had the copyright. The latter agreed to do whatever Newman wished in the matter.[16] Copeland consented to be editor and negotiated with Rivingtons to have the sermons republished. Rivington agreed to pay £20 after the sale of the first 500 copies, plus £4 for every 100 additional copies.[17] The volumes began to appear in 1868 and were an

[11]Ibid., XVI, 19-20, 28, 30.

[12]Ibid., XVI, 29, n. 2.

[13]Among the Rivington correspondence, B.O. All correspondence referred to in subsequent notes is at the Birmingham Oratory Archives.

[14]*Letters and diaries*, XXV, 254.

[15]The controversy centered around an alteration of a verse in the *Christian Year*, which, in accordance with Keble's wishes, was made in a posthumous edition. Sir John Coleridge, in defending the right and duty of Keble's heirs to make the alterations, remarked: "While Dr. Newman remained in our Church he published six volumes of Parochial sermons and one of Plain Sermons, invaluable contributions to her pastoral literature; he refuses now, it is said, to order or allow a mere reprint of them. Thousands regret this, but can any just man complain of unfair dealing, or censure him as doing an immoral act?" (ibid., XXIII, 36, n. 2).

[16]Ibid., XXIII, 36; letter to Froude, ibid., XXIII, 37.

[17]Ibid., XXIII, 387, n. 1.

enormous success, especially among Nonconformists, more than
twenty thousand being sold by the end of 1869.[18] By the middle
of July 1868, a sum of £1,000 was due and Newman, in a letter to
Copeland, said: "As to the money, give me what you please. It will
be *your gift.*"[19] This success prompted Rivington to reprint
Sermons bearing on subjects of the day in 1869, which proved so
popular that it was reissued in 1871, 1873, 1879, and 1885.[20]

When Pickering brought out Newman's *Two essays on miracles*
in 1870, Rivington was annoyed that it had the same binding and
color as the *Parochial and plain sermons.*[21] Newman mentioned
this to Copeland, who thought that Rivington might be resentful
at not having been offered Newman's other Anglican works for
republication, specifically his reviews which he was now going to
publish with Pickering as *Essays critical and historical.*[22] Newman
replied:

As to the Reviews, when Pickering proposed it to me, I said 1. that *I*
believed they were Rivingtons' property and that, since they were *controversial*, (which the Sermons were not) I could not republish them without
adding (on the Audi alteram partem principle) answers to their Anti-Roman
arguments. He showed me that the copy right was mine, not Rivingtons!
From various occurrences, during the last 20 or 30 years, I was, and am, quite
sure that Rivingtons will not publish any thing Roman. E.g. to go back a
long way, in 1844, they asked me for a new edition of my 'Prophetical
Office.' I answered 'yes, on condition that I might state in what respects I had
abandoned what I had advanced in the volume.' This put an end to the
negociations. The same animus has shown itself again and again up to this
time. However, I *did* indirectly offer them the 'Reviews'. I wrote to tell them
that I thought of republishing them—that I believed the copy right was mine,
but I asked them if it was, and that, if I republished, I should add *answers* to
my Anti-Roman arguments advanced in them. I was quite sure that this would
be a spoke in the wheel—however, I was quite *open* to any advance on their
part, if they chose to make me an offer. They answered 'Yes—that the copy
right *was* mine, *and* they would be obliged if Mr Pickering would not use

[18]Ibid., XXIV, 177, n. 1, and 304, n. 1. A total of 19,800 copies were sold by
July 1, 1869.

[19]Ibid., XXIV, 177.

[20]Ibid., XXIV, 177, n. 1, and 186, n. 1.

[21]Ibid., XXV, 240-41, 243-44.

[22]Ibid., XXV, 247, n. 2.

their coloured cover to his edition of my 'Miracles'.' Not a word, as to their taking the publishing of my Reviews, (which I certainly did not expect.) . . . I thought and think that they never would take my Reviews with the *necessary* new additions to them. This being the case, what have I done wrong? . . . He only took the new Edition of my Parochial Sermons, because they came from you, not me.[23]

In September 1871 Newman asked Copeland to find out whether Rivington would take the expenses of an edition of the Oxford University *Sermons*, in which he would put notes.[24] Copeland wrote to Newman on October 5 that Rivington agreed to publish a new edition "with such notes as you may see fit as Editor to insert or append," uniform with *Parochial and plain sermons*, and on the same terms.[25] It appeared in 1872, and was reprinted in 1880, 1884, 1887, and 1890. Encouraged by its sale in 1872, Newman wrote Copeland, February 21, 1873: "As the University Sermons sell fairly well, I shall in the course of another year, if I live, ask the R[ivington]s to take my 'Justification.' "[26] They did, and *Lectures on justification* was republished in 1874. The rest of Newman's Anglican works, however, were republished by Pickering, with whom Newman had more cordial dealings.

Burns, Lambert, and Oates

The firm was started by James Burns (1808–1871), who, when employed by Whitaker & Co. in 1832, succeeded so quickly in learning the business that in 1834 he set himself up as publisher and bookseller, first in Duke Street, Manchester Square, and then at 17 Portman Street, Portman Square. He published two important series: The Englishman's Library, and The Fireside Library, as well as *Poems and pictures*, 1845, the first of the illustrated Christmas books. Although originally Presbyterian, he became a Tractarian and was converted to Catholicism in 1847. His conver-

[23]Ibid., XXV, 247-48.

[24]Ibid., XXV, 403.

[25]Letter of Copeland to N, Oct. 5, 1871, Rivington correspondence.

[26]*Letters and diaries*, XXVI, 256.

sion created a stir, with people writing to him to stay in the
Church of England. Lambert joined the firm around 1849 or 1850
and William Wilfrid Oates, in 1865. The firm published the *Annals
of the Propagation of the Faith*, starting in 1861, and the *Dublin
Review*, starting in 1863.[27]

Newman's relations with Burns began with the publication of
Loss and gain (1848), which was written specifically to aid Burns,
whose business Newman feared might suffer because of his conversion.[28] Newman had to undertake the publication at his own
risk.[29] The work sold enough to warrant a smaller second edition
in the same year. In 1849 Newman issued under Burns's imprint a
fourth edition of *Parochial sermons*, vol. IV, with the text, as he
said in the preface, "so far altered as they contained any thing
contrary to Faith and Morals." Five hundred copies were printed.
The work sold well in the beginning but was never reprinted. This
was the only corrected copy of Newman's Anglican sermons that
was ever republished.

In 1850 Burns published Newman's *Lectures on certain
difficulties felt by Anglicans in submitting to the Catholic Church*,
Newman bearing the cost of printing. On March 22 he sent Newman £100 in payment. Cardinal Wiseman was annoyed at the
dearness of the lectures, which, he said, prevented leading
Catholics from giving away large numbers of them. Newman took
this as a compliment to the lectures. In a letter to Faber, July 31,
1851, he asserted: *"They are cheaper than last year.* Then they
were 1/per 27 pages, now 1/per 34. I printed two thousand of
my St. Chad's Sermon [*Christ upon the waters*], and *lost by the
2000.* If there is a *demand* for cheap, I will sell cheap, hitherto
cheap does *not pay expences.*"[30] In the same year he published
with Burns his *Lectures on the present position of Catholics in*

---

[27] Frederick Boase, *Modern English biography*, and Joseph Gillow, *Bibliographical
dictionary of the English Catholics.*

[28] *Letters and diaries*, XXVIII, 264.

[29] Ibid., XIII, 194 and n. 1.

[30] Ibid., XIV, 321-22.

England, which involved him in the famous libel suit with Achilli.[31]
Newman wanted a cheap edition to sell at 3d. per pamphlet as
well as the regular one which was selling at 1s. 3d., but Burns re-
jected this, so Newman had the cheap edition published in
Birmingham.[32]

In 1853 Burns wrote Newman about a new series of popular
books on Catholicism which he hoped to publish and asked him if
he would contribute to it.[33] It became known as the Popular
Catholic Library, edited by J. M. Capes, J. S. Northcote, and
E. M. Thompson. This may have stimulated Newman to take up
work again on *Callista*, which he had begun in 1849. Since this
work, which appeared in 1856, was given to Burns to help him out
commercially, Burns could reprint it without Newman's permission, in lots usually of one thousand, for which Newman received
the small sum of £10.[34] His initial royalty seems to have been
£30.[35] The book went well, having sold 9,500 copies by July
1872.[36] Though Newman was not always pleased with Burns's
handling of his works, the latter was adept in arranging foreign
editions and translations. In September 1857 Newman received
the payment of £20 for the French translation of *Callista*.[37] In
the same year Burns published Newman's *Sermons on various
occasions*. Since the initial printing was only 500 copies, a new
printing was necessary by November, and it came out the following
year.

In 1858 Newman apparently made his first attempt to produce
a uniform edition of his works among all his publishers, by having
each firm put out books of equal size and with a similar binding.
Longmans forwarded copies of their works to Burns for binding

----

[31]See Vincent Ferrer Blehl, S.J., "Newman on Trial," *The Month*, XXVII (Feb.
1962), 69-80, for an account of this episode.

[32]*Letters and diaries*, XIV, 311 and n. 2.

[33]Letter of Burns to N, Dec. 29, 1853.

[34]*Letters and diaries*, XXVI, 129.

[35]Ibid., XVIII, 485.

[36]Ibid., XXVI, 129, n. 3.

[37]Letter of Burns to N, Sept. 9, 1857.

in 1859. In the intervening years between 1858 and 1865 *Callista* and *Loss and gain* continued to be reprinted as need required. In 1865 Burns issued *The dream of Gerontius*, which had originally been published in the *Month*. It was a great success and probably ran through more impressions than any other work, being reprinted twenty-seven times by 1890. In 1886 it had to be reset because the plates had worn out. It was ordered for nearly every prison in England, and General Gordon meditated on it before his death at Khartoum.[38]

In April 1867 Burns raised Newman's royalty on each thousand of *Callista* from £10 to £15.[39] In the same year he published a new edition of *The Church of the Fathers* (which was previously published by Duffy), but the most significant event was the publication of *Verses on various occasions*, which sold very rapidly. In April 1869 Newman was sent £179 15s. 5d. for the sale of the work.[40]

The year 1870 saw the publication of one of Newman's major works, *An essay in aid of a grammar of assent,* but only after Burns reassured Newman that he would promote it as well as Longmans.[41] Newman had, by this time, been dealing with Pickering and evidently had some doubts about the ability of Catholic publishers to push sales of those of his works which would be of interest to non-Catholic booksellers and readers. By June 20, the supply was down to 370 copies, and 250 were printed as a stopgap measure before corrections were made.[42] In September Burns sent Newman £100 in account on it.[43] He also arranged to have it published in America, for which Newman received a payment of £30.[44] In this year also Newman began to employ a new printer,

[38] Letter of Oates to N, May 7, 1880; Ward, II, 357, 514-15.

[39] Letter of Burns to N, April 17, 1867.

[40] Letter of Burns and Oates to N, April 9, 1869.

[41] Letter of Burns to N, Jan. 17, 1870.

[42] Letter of Oates to N, June 20, 1870.

[43] Letter of Burns to N, Sept. 9, 1870.

[44] Letter of Burns and Oates to N, July 7, 1870.

Ballantyne of Edinburgh, but Gilbert and Rivington continued to be employed at intervals, so that the break was not complete. Also it was agreed that accounts would be settled in March on sales to the previous December, instead, as they had previously done, to settle them on each work as editions went out of print. Accordingly, in March 1871 Newman was paid £583 17s. 11d.[45] This year Burns died and the business was run by William Wilfrid Oates, who became Newman's regular correspondent.

On December 29, 1871, Oates wrote that he would be happy to print 1,000 copies of the *Present position of Catholics*, which had last been published by Duffy in 1857, "at my expense and account to you in the same way as if you printed it at your expense. I feel pretty sure there would be a balance in favor of the work by December 1872." On June 2, 1872, he informed Newman that *Certain difficulties felt by Anglicans* was out of print: "I shall be happy to take it on the same terms as the last—that is, to bear all risk till the edition is paid for."[46] Whether Newman agreed to these terms is not clear, since in a letter of July 5, 1872, to Oates, Newman informed him that "I have this day paid Messrs Ballantyne their account for printing the 'Present position of Catholics.' I shall do the same with the 'Difficulties of Anglicans—.' "[47]

No new major work of Newman was subsequently published by the firm, only reprints of the old. In March 1873 an account was settled for £176 9s. 5d.[48]

In December 1876 William Wilfrid Oates died, and his son Wilfrid carried on the business. In July 1882 an account was settled for £285 2s. 7d. and in 1883 for £291 5s. 4d.[49] In 1884 Newman began to sound out each of his publishers on what they would offer for the copyrights of his works. On March 17, 1884, Oates made an offer of £1,000 cash and "say an annual sum

---

[45] Letter of Oates to N, Nov. 8, 1870; letter of Burns and Oates to N, March 24, 1871.

[46] Letters of Oates to N, Dec. 29, 1871, June 2, 1872.

[47] *Letters and diaries*, XXVI, 131.

[48] Letter of Oates to N, March 22, 1873.

[49] Letters of Oates to N, July 11, 1882, June 30, 1883.

besides like £100 per year."[50] Newman did not accept it, and in early 1885 he withdrew several of his works from Burns and Oates and sold them to Longmans.

James Duffy

James Duffy (1808 or 1809–1871), beginning as a peddler in Cavan, became a publisher of religious books in Dublin and later of those of the Young Irelanders. His business was at 7 Wellington Quay, which he eventually built up with a trade extending to America, India, and Australia.[51]

Newman's connection with Duffy began in a rather interesting way in May 1852 when he was delivering his lectures on university education in Dublin. He gives an account of it in a letter to a fellow Oratorian, John Joseph Gordon: "You will accuse me of all manner of crimes, when you learn that I have *given away* my first edition of 2500 copies (of 12 Lectures) to Duffy the Publisher. It is a long story to tell how I was forced to it by the excitable Mac Cabe, who professing . . . 'veneration' for me, said I was committing a 'breach of *good faith*,' because I complied with Lucas's wish, (as I should, if asked, have complied with *his*,) to put the Discourse in his Newspaper [*The Tablet*]. I found I should be Anti-Irish etc etc. so I *literally* have given Duffy the edition. They are to be published at /6." Ambrose St. John, another Oratorian and close friend of Newman, replied on May 14, "We pretty generally agree that you did right in giving Duffy the lectures . . . but I don't see why you should not take what he thinks fit to give you." "There is no record that Duffy ever thought fit to give Newman anything, but the lectures were nicely printed in octavo, each one about a week after delivery."[52]

In the next year Newman turned to Duffy to take over the stock of *Lectures on certain difficulties of Anglicans* and *Lectures on the present position of Catholics in England* from Burns, when

[50]Letter of Oates to N, March 14, 1884.

[51]*Letters and diaries*, XV, 558.

[52]Ibid., XV, 86 and n. 4.

the latter would not pay Newman.[53] In the same year Duffy put out an edition of *Loss and gain* and *Verses on religious subjects.* In 1854 he published Newman's *Lectures on the history of the Turks,* of which, Newman said in a letter, "I think *that*, the first year, payed its expenses and £14 over, or thereabouts. And £14 to £16 the second year?"[54] In 1856 Duffy offered Newman £100 for the two volumes of *Lectures* on Anglicanism and Catholicism, which the latter evidently used to pay for the cost of printing a reduced version of *The Church of the Fathers.* These three works were published by Duffy in 1857.[55] In 1862, Newman returned to Duffy to have him republish the *Discourses to mixed congregations*, originally published by Longmans but out of print since 1860.

Basil Montagu Pickering

Basil Montagu Pickering (1835–1878) was the only son of William Pickering, the publisher, who died in 1854, and whose premises were from 1842 onward at 177 Piccadilly. The business was taken over by James Toovey, who employed the young Pickering. In 1858 Pickering set up on his own as a publisher and dealer in rare books, at 196 Piccadilly. He published poems by Swinburne, 1860, J. H. Frere's *Works*, 1872, and a facsimile of the first edition of *Paradise lost*, 1873.[56]

Newman's connection with Pickering began when he received a letter dated December 18, 1868, informing him that the firm had just purchased from the proprietors of the *Encyclopaedia metropolitana* the copyright of Newman's *Life of Apollonius Tyanaeus with a comparison of the miracles of scripture*, as well as copies of them. He wanted to know whether he had a right to sell them. Though Newman had always claimed the copyright, he did not

[53]Ibid., XVII, 363.

[54]Ibid., XVII, 367.

[55]Ibid., XVII, 366-67.

[56]*Dictionary of national biography.*

know, as he informed Pickering, what the law was on the matter.[57]
On April 17, 1869, in acknowledging the receipt of a copy of his
Apollonius Tyanaeus from Pickering, Newman suggested that the
two subjects, a Life and an Essay, "do not hang well together"
and asked whether Pickering would consider leaving out the Life
and adding his other essay on ecclesiastical miracles in one volume.[58] Pickering agreed to do so and published *Two essays on
scripture miracles and on ecclesiastical* in 1870, in a volume which
Newman thought "a very handsome one." In size, type, lettering,
and coloring it matched the new Copeland edition of his *Parochial
and plain sermons.*[59] From this time on Newman arranged to have
his publishers produce uniform editions of his works. Moreover,
to Newman's surprise, 800 out of 1,000 copies were sold as of
November 9, for which Pickering sent a check of £18, half of the
profits. Newman expressed a hope that Pickering had been fair to
himself, since he had taken "all the risk."[60] Pickering now showed
an interest in republishing other writings of Newman and correspondence on the matter led eventually to the republication of his
reviews as *Essays critical and historical,* 1871, *Discussions and
arguments,* 1872, and *Historical sketches,* 3 vols., 1872, 1873.

Meanwhile, Rivingtons were annoyed, as previously noted, that
Newman had chosen the same binding and color for *Miracles* as
for the *Parochial and plain sermons.* Newman thought it a compliment to them, and that it would promote the sale of the sermons
as well as the *Miracles* if they seemed like portions of a series.
"But they exhibit a dry grumpiness about it, which is marvellous.
I have written to them in the honestest and sweetest manner about
it, but they answer in the tone of a chisel."[61] Newman had already
sounded out Pickering on republishing his reviews, and a letter to
Pickering at this time reveals Newman's publishing problems:

[57]*Letters and diaries,* XXIV, 190 and n. 2, 191.

[58]Ibid., XXIV, 243.

[59]Ibid., XXV, 21, 155, 190.

[60]Ibid., XXV, 228.

[61]Ibid., XXV, 243.

I sent your letter to me to Messrs Rivington and they have acknowledged it this morning. I cannot think what makes them so cross. I told them I was going to publish the Reviews with you, and gave a good reason, why I could not publish with them, viz that I was going to add notes in answer to my Anglican arguments, and because such notes they never could accept. And, as *they* could not publish my notes, so *I* could not omit them—so that to publish with them is impossible.

Nor is it possible for me to publish them with Messrs Burns—because, as Messrs Rivingtons would not accept the Catholic portion of the volumes, so Burns could not publish the Anglican, without getting into trouble with Catholics.

You see then what works I can re-publish with you—those which have both Anglican and Catholic arguments. This will show you how little I thought you a 'Protestant publisher.'[62]

On January 21, 1871, Newman acknowledged a check from Pickering for £40 14s. with a note that the *Miracles* had sold very quickly.[63] *Essays critical and historical* sold rapidly enough to go into a second printing to which Newman added corrections. Newman wrote to Matthew Arnold that he was sending him a copy of *Discussions and arguments* by way of "showing you the gratitude, which I sincerely feel, for the various instances of your kindness towards me." Arnold wrote to ask if he would endorse the copy, which Newman did and received in reply a letter saying: "I find your book with its kind inscription awaiting me here on my return home, after a period of much family trouble. To read you, always gives me high pleasure; and it always carries me back, besides, to some of the happiest places and times of my life; so the book is particularly welcome to me just now."[64]

The correspondence with Pickering for the year 1872 is taken up with the preparation of *Historical sketches*, which were not published in the order in which Newman wanted them to be eventually placed. The confusion that resulted from this is discussed in the note placed at the beginning of *Historical sketches* in the bibliography. In one letter to Pickering, Newman mentions that he sees that the New York *Catholic World* says that "you are 'the

[62]Ibid., XXV, 243-44.
[63]Ibid., XXV, 271.
[64]Ibid., XXVI, 20 and n. 3.

pink of elegant and aristocratic publishers.' I hope this means they do not mean to reprint and undersell you in America."[65]

In 1873 Newman decided to reprint in one volume his *Discourses on university education*, the second edition of which was still in stock with Longmans, together with *Lectures and essays on university subjects*, also published by Longmans. He gave it the title *Idea of a university*. He also approached Pickering regarding what became in 1874 *Tracts theological and ecclesiastical*, copies of which he had sent to Pusey and Bright of Christ Church, Oxford, to Copeland, and to others.[66] But the major venture of these years was the publication of *A letter to the duke of Norfolk* in 1875, which was an instant success. By midsummer Pickering paid Newman a total of £500 on its sale. Newman was pleased, and in a letter of August 7 thanked Pickering for his "zeal and care" in the management of the work.[67] In the same year Pickering purchased from Lumley the copyright of *The Arians*, which Lumley had published as a third edition in 1871 with the corrections and notes Newman had always wanted to add to it. Pickering's edition came out in 1876. In the same year Newman decided to take the *Letter to Pusey* which had appeared in Burns, Oates's volume of *Difficulties of Anglicans* and put it into a volume with the *Letter to the duke of Norfolk* to be published by Pickering. Both volumes bore the same general title, *Certain difficulties of Anglicans*, but since each volume could be read and sold separately, neither volume was marked volume 1 or volume 2; however, one asterisk was affixed to what later became volume 1, this published by Burns, Oates, and two asterisks to what became volume 2, published by Pickering, and they were advertised as "first series" and "second series," respectively.

In 1877 Newman published with Pickering the *Via media* in two volumes, the first containing his Anglican *Lectures on the prophetical office of the Church* and the second comprised of tracts and writings dealing with the Oxford movement. Since the

[65]Ibid., XXVI, 161.

[66]Letter of N to Pickering, March 16, 1874; *Letters and diaries*, XXVII, 36.

[67]*Letters and diaries*, XXVII, 340.

two volumes were not interdependent, the volumes were issued
separately, volume 1 first in order to serve as an advertisement for
volume 2. At this time Newman set to work on a thorough revision
of his *Essay on the development of Christian doctrine*, in which he
rearranged the order of the chapters and added entire paragraphs.
Pickering's letters during this year take on a more personal note,
in which he speaks of illness and family troubles. What these were
is not entirely clear from the correspondence, but on March 15 he
wrote: "The continued anxiety all through 1876 & the terrible
termination to it, losing wife & all remaining children within one
month has left me so prostrate that every exertion has been a
trouble, this with cold upon cold & enlarged glands which I fear
may break & cause trouble, has caused me to neglect much that
I ought to have done."[68] But these troubles apparently did only
minor harm to his handling of Newman's affairs, though in this
year the trouble about the numbering of *Historical sketches*
reached a peak.

Early in 1878 Pickering died and James Toovey became
executor, and Alexander D. Denny bought the business in April.
The administration of Newman's affairs passed into the hands of
Alfred Cutter, who had been and remained chief clerk at the firm.
He managed all the corrections and proof for the *Essay*, which was
ready by March. Toovey meanwhile took an inventory of Newman's volumes in stock at Pickering and gave the following account
in two letters to Newman, May 14 and 17, 1878.[69]

Work	No. Printed	Quires	Bound
A. Works of which copyrights and stereoplates were owned half by Pickering, half by Newman			
Discussions 2nd ed.	500	none	20
Miracles	500	200	100
Essays, 2 vols.	500	250	27
Sketches, vol. 1	500	400	70
" vol. 2	500	—	100
" vol. 3	500	300	114

[68]Letter of Pickering to N, March 15, 1876.
[69]Letter of Toovey to N, May 14, 1878.

Work	No. Printed	Quires	Bound
B. Works owned by Newman, published on commission by Pickering			
Via Media, vol. 1	1,000	200	49
" " vol. 2	1,000	400	7
Idea of a University	500	300	58
Callista	500	300	27
Tracts	1,000	90	70
Diff. of Anglic. (II)	1,000	615	217
Devel. of Doctrine	—	—	—

The Arians, which was stereotyped, was owned by Pickering, who paid a royalty to Newman. The *Idea of a university* was also stereotyped. In 1873 Newman printed a new and larger edition of *Callista* to be uniform with his other works and wanted to give it to Pickering because he thought Burns had never been able to sell it to the Protestant market. Oates protested and Newman allowed him to publish the new edition but with Pickering's name also on the title page.[70] The same was true of the 1876 edition referred to above. *Loss and gain* was likewise printed with Pickering's name on it in 1874.

At this time Newman decided to buy back all his copyrights except that of *The Arians* and paid £79 9s. 8d. for the stereo-plates.[71] All works, except *The Arians*, were henceforth published solely on a commission basis. At this time also, with the reprinting of "The Turks," vol. 1 (formerly **) of *Historical sketches*, Pickering's system of asterisks was abandoned. Plans were discussed in 1879 and 1880 to prepare a general index to all of Newman's works, but this in the event was never realized.

In 1880 a contract was signed for the publication of *Select treatises of St. Athanasius*, which involved the retranslation of many passages in the earlier edition in the Library of the Fathers, and the work was published in the following year. In 1880–81, reprints, binding sets, and adjustments in a number of Newman's works put his account in deficit. As a result, in July 1881 he owed

[70]*Letters and diaries*, XXVI, 307; see also pp. 129, 312.

[71]Letters of Denny to N, May 29 and June 4, 1878.

Denny £121 6s. 1d.[72] In 1881 volumes II and III of *Historical sketches, Essays critical and historical* and *Tracts theological and ecclesiastical* with changes shortly to be mentioned, *Two essays on miracles*, and the *Idea* were reprinted. The note appended to the "Theology of St. Ignatius" in *Essays* was dropped and "Apostolic tradition" was added as Essay III. The former, called "On the text of the seven epistles of St. Ignatius," was added to the second edition of *Tracts*, to which was also added "The ordo de tempore in the breviary." This involved considerable trouble for the printer, who had to make the changes in the plates.

In 1882 volume I of *Historical sketches, Discussions and arguments*, and *The Arians* were reprinted. What arrangements were made with Burns and Oates on the latter I do not know, but this edition, marked the fifth though it was probably a corrected impression, since the work was stereoplated, carries no date, has Burns & Oates on the title page, and Pickering on the spine. In this year accounts, which since Pickering's death were settled twice a year, showed a balance in February of £52 14s. 7d. and in August of £126 17s. 9d.[73] Also, Newman suggested that Denny settle his accounts only once a year.[74]

In 1884 relations between Newman and the firm deteriorated. Newman was considering selling his copyrights. He mentions that he had been given an offer by a firm, though he does not specify the name, to publish on a royalty basis. Denny replied, "I do not think a royalty would bring Your Eminence so much profit as the present system, under which your works are published, by which you get all the profit except the commission of 10% on sales."[75] In another letter, Newman informed Denny that he had been made a specific offer to publish on a royalty basis.[76] On October 30 Denny offered to take the responsibility for publication on himself and to pay Newman one shilling for every volume sold. On

---

[72]Letter of Denny to N, July 30, 1878.

[73]Letters of Denny to N, Feb. 7 and Aug. 11, 1882.

[74]Letter of N to Denny, Aug. 16, 1882.

[75]Letter of Denny to N, Oct. 22, 1884.

[76]*Letters and diaries*, XXX, 421.

November 27 Newman replied that he had given up the idea of selling his books on a royalty basis.

The year 1885 saw the effective end of the business association between Newman and Denny. On January 20, Newman wrote to Denny saying that he had received a more advantageous offer than the one Denny had proposed and he had definitely accepted it. Thus the books were withdrawn from Pickering, except for *The Arians*, since Denny owned the copyright, and given to Longmans. On March 16, Denny sent Newman a check for £143 17s. 8d. In September 1886 Newman bought back the copyright, stereotype, and stock of *The Arians*.

Longmans

The firm was started by Thomas Longman (1699–1755), the publisher of the third volume of Hume's first work, *Treatise of human nature*, in 1740. He was also one of the six booksellers who entered into an agreement with Samuel Johnson for the production of his dictionary. He was succeeded by his nephew Thomas (1730–1797), who in turn was succeeded by his son Thomas Norton Longman (1771–1842). The latter took Owen Rees into partnership, making the firm one of the greatest in London, the publishers for Wordsworth, Southey, Scott, and Moore and in 1826 the sole proprietor of the *Edinburgh Review*. Thomas (1804–1879), son of Thomas Norton, became a partner in 1834, publishing for Macaulay and Disraeli, and in 1839 William (1813–1877), his younger brother, became a partner.[77] Newman's correspondence was with William until his death in 1877 and then with William's son, Charles J. Longman, who became a member of the firm in the same year. Of the other partners who came and went, Green remained the longest.

Newman's first book to be published with the firm was the *Discourses addressed to mixed congregations* in 1849. It was at his own expense, Longmans taking a commission of 10 percent. In February 1850 Newman was informed that 750 copies had been

---

[77]*Dictionary of national biography.*

sold and a new edition was needed.[78] Another printing of 1,000 copies was made, and Longmans advised Newman that the law being uncertain, it would be better to register the new edition at Stationers Hall, even though the copyright subsisted in the author independently of registration.[79] The second edition did not sell rapidly, for there were 387 copies in stock as of December 20, 1852, and 239 as of March 3, 1855. By September 1860 the stock was sold out and Longmans asked if Newman wanted to reprint it, suggesting in that event 500 or even 250 copies.[80] Newman later wrote a memorandum on the latter: "I did not act upon this, thinking that I shd have to lay out money now, & might die before the edition ran out." Newman later wanted Burns to publish it at Burns's risk and pay him in advance, but Burns replied, March 2, 1862, "these are not times when we can pay in advance for books," and so the work was republished by Duffy in the same year.

In 1856 Longmans agreed to publish at Newman's risk his *Office and work of universities* and in 1859 his *Lectures and essays on university subjects*, as well as a cut-down second edition of the *Discourses on university education*, retitled the *Scope and nature of university education*. The most important of Newman's works to be published by Longmans, however, was the *Apologia*, in 1864, first in pamphlet form of seven parts and an appendix, and then in bound form. Financially and in every other way it represented a turning point in Newman's publishing ventures. By October, Longmans owed him £2,000.[81] In a letter of November 12, 1864, Longmans wrote that the sale of the complete work continued but the sale of the separate parts was very small. The firm proposed to print such numbers as would convert the stock into complete sets, which would give 250 plus the 180 that were on hand. The letter continued: "By March we will sell all. The point for your consideration, therefore, is whether you will continue to publish the book in its present form, or whether you will,

---

[78]Letters of Longman and Brown to N, Feb. 15 and 20, 1850.

[79]Letter of Longman and Brown to N, Dec. 17, 1850.

[80]Letters of William Longman to N, Sept. 5 and 21, 1860.

[81]Letter of William Longman to N, Oct. 3, 1864.

after a certain time, issue it in a smaller form, omitting perhaps, such passages or parts of the work as derive their interest from the controversy. I cannot but think that this would be the best course."

Newman followed this advice in his second edition, which he published in 1865 under the title *History of my religious opinions.* On December 13, 1867 Longmans expressed regrets that Newman "did not receive in due course our cheque for £104/15/9." The edition was sold out in 1869, and Newman issued new impressions with additional notes in 1869 and 1870 which were sold out by November 1872.[82] A new impression was ready by January 16, 1873, when the work returned to its original title, *Apologia pro vita sua*, Newman adding the subtitle *Being a history of his religious opinions.*

In the interim period Newman had published with Longmans his *Letter to Pusey* in 1866, which went through three editions in one year. In 1872 he decided to take it, the *Lectures and essays on university subjects,* and the second edition of *Scope and nature of universities* out of Longmans' hands, the *Letter to Pusey* to be conjoined with *Lectures on certain difficulties of Anglicans* published by Burns and the other two to be conjoined in the *Idea of a university*, to be published by Pickering. He first asked Pickering's advice whether he ought to inform Longmans about his republishing the *Letter to Pusey*, since it might interfere with the sales of the remaining copies of Longmans' third edition. Pickering replied that since Newman had met the expense of his pamphlet and since it occupied little storage space, Longmans would have no claim on him.[83] Accordingly Newman wrote a formal letter to William Longman, July 6, 1872:

> I propose to add my 'Letter to Dr Pusey', which you were so good as to publish for me in 1866 to a new edition of my 'Anglican Difficulties' of which Messrs Burns and Oates have the sale. This is in consequence of my aiming at making a uniform edition of all that I have written, and the 'Letter' cannot of itself make a volume.

---

[82]Letters of Longmans to N, Jan. 29 and March 20, 1869, Dec. 3, 1872.

[83]*Letters and diaries*, XXVI, 118 and n. 3.

You gave me advice some years ago, which I followed, not to print a second edition of my 'Lectures and Essays on Universities subject [*sic*],' which you had published for me in 1859, under the belief that it would not pay its expenses. Since it was out of print it has been called for in various quarters. I observe also that the second edition of my 'Scope and Nature of Universities,' (which you did me the favour of undertaking, though the first edition was published in Ireland), at the time of your last statement (though published in 1859) out of 1000 copies, had still copies in hand.

It seems to me that from the large field which your publishing transactions occupy, second editions can hardly have a place in them; nor do I feel I can undertake them myself with the risk of a loss. This leads me to think that in the uniform edition I speak of, I had better not trouble you with these two volumes.

I am glad to see the Apologia still sells, and justifies your recommendations to me, on the second edition, to have it stereotyped. You have taken a great interest in it from the first.[84]

On October 25, 1873, Longmans wrote Newman, "Can you send a small supply of the Office and work of universities, say about 25 copies, or is the work to be considered out of print?" Newman replied, October 27: "In answer to your question I beg to say I have no intention of reprinting the 'Office and Work etc' in the shape in which you did me the favour of publishing it. It was one of the books to which I referred in the conversation I had with Mr William Longman in July 1872, which I am grouping under more general titles and publishing with Mr Pickering as part of a Series."[85]

Prior to this, on May 14, 1873, Longmans wrote that the firm wanted to return 425 copies of the 454 on hand of *The pope and the revolution*, since only 2 copies had been sold in the past year. In December, Newman's account was £51 14s. 9d. and in December 1874, £59 4s. 2d.[86] Five hundred more copies of the *Apologia* had to be printed in 1875 and again in 1876.[87] In 1878, when the stock was exhausted, Newman added additional notes

[84]Ibid., XXVI, 132.

[85]Ibid., XXVI, 380.

[86]Letters of Longmans to N, Dec. 4, 1873, Dec. 4, 1874.

[87]Letter of William Longman to N, March 1, 1875; letters of Longmans to N, Oct. 2, 1876, and May 6, 1878.

to the new edition, but it was not so marked, though Longmans pointed out that "it is not called *new edition* on the *title page*. Is this as you wish?"[88] As of December 3, 1878, Newman's account was £57 16s. 3d. By March 18, of the next year 750 more copies needed to be reprinted and by October 23 only 250 copies remained, Longmans suggesting that another 750 copies be reprinted. The increased sales showed in Newman's account for this year, which was £105 2s. 6d.[89] The sales slipped in 1880, Newman receiving £94 5s. 9d.[90] Five hundred copies were reprinted in June 1881, of which only 12 copies remained by July 1882, when a new reprint was made.[91] By June the next year the stock was low and Longmans asked to reprint 750 copies.[92]

In 1884 Newman began seriously to think of selling his copyrights. He corresponded with Burns, Pickering, and Rivington. Meanwhile he consulted Lord Coleridge, who informed Charles Longman of his intent. This led Longman to make an offer, after a rough evaluation of the works based on information supplied by Newman, to take them for something between £2,500 and £3,000, not including the rights to two books put out by Kegan Paul.[93] On July 4 Newman abruptly informed Longman that he had "no intention of pursuing the inquiry further," offered to reimburse him for any expense he may have caused, and asked for the return of "various documents" which he had sent. Longman expressed his regrets at the negative termination of negotiations and told Newman that there were no expenses involved.[94]

On January 2, 1885, Charles Longman wrote saying that the *Apologia* should be reprinted at once, and he suggested that 1,250 copies be printed instead of 750. Newman felt he would never get back his expenses and asked if Longman would advise selling the

[88] Letter of Longmans to N, July 16, 1878.

[89] Letter of Longmans to N, Dec. 4, 1879.

[90] Letter of Longmans to N, Dec. 4, 1880.

[91] Letter of Longmans to N, July 10, 1882.

[92] Letter of C. J. Longman to N, June 22, 1883.

[93] Letter of C. J. Longman to N, July 2, 1884.

[94] Letter of C. J. Longman to N, July 5, 1884.

copyright according to an offer he had or to accept a royalty on it.[95] Longman in reply offered (1) that the stereoplates be placed at the firm's disposal free of charge; (2) that it pay the entire cost of printing, etc.; (3) that it pay one-fourth the retail price of all copies sold, the royalties on each edition to be paid in advance, on publication. Consequently, on a new edition of 750 copies, the royalties would be £56 5s. Newman would also have the right to make small corrections.[96] Newman accepted and on January 15, asked if Longman would be interested in giving royalties on other works he was publishing on commission. Longman replied that he would, on the same basis as the *Apologia* depending upon the stock. The works in question were the *Idea of a university, Historical sketches*, 3 vols., *Discussions and arguments*, and *An essay on the development of doctrine*—all published by Pickering. On February 2, Longman offered £250 for the stock of these volumes, which he later reduced to £84 15s. 6d. because of a mistake in the counting of the copies of the *Essay on development.* In a second letter on February 3 Newman said that it would be a relief to him if Longman would take all the volumes that were stereoplated. After some investigation of what was and what was not stereo-plated, Longman offered £300 for the existing stock of the *Essays on miracles, Essays critical and historical*, 2 vols., *Via media*, 2 vols., which were already stereoplated, and two volumes of *Certain difficulties of Anglicans* and the *Grammar of assent*, which would be stereoplated at Newman's expense.[97] Newman accepted, and accordingly £300 was sent by Longmans on March 7. Eventually Longmans acquired the copyrights to all Newman's works.

In summing up Newman's publishing activity, certain conclusions may be easily drawn. First, Newman for the most part, especially after 1845, paid for the printing of his works, the publishers selling them on commission, generally at 10 percent. Second, Newman made relatively little money on his publications until the time of the *Apologia.* Third, the most cordial and cooperative of the pub-

[95]Letter of N to C. J. Longman, Jan. 8, 1885.

[96]Letter of C. J. Longman to N, Jan. 13, 1885.

[97]Letter of C. J. Longman to N, Feb. 23, 1885.

lishers was Pickering, to whom Newman was indebted for the republication of many of his works. Newman's relations with his publishers may not be the most exciting or interesting aspect of his biography, but the correspondence provides a vivid insight into the perennial problems that engage both publisher and author.

John Henry Newman
A Bibliographical Catalogue
of His Writings

APOLOGIA PRO VITA SUA:

BEING

A Reply to a Pamphlet

ENTITLED

" WHAT, THEN, DOES DR. NEWMAN MEAN?"

" Commit thy way to the Lord, and trust in Him, and He will do it.
And He will bring forth thy justice as the light, and thy judgment as the noon-day."

BY JOHN HENRY NEWMAN, D.D.

LONDON:
LONGMAN, GREEN, LONGMAN, ROBERTS, AND GREEN.
1864.

A1a

DISCOURSES

ON

THE SCOPE AND NATURE

OF

UNIVERSITY EDUCATION

ADDRESSED TO

THE CATHOLICS OF DUBLIN.

BY

JOHN HENRY NEWMAN, D.D.,
PRESIDENT OF THE CATHOLIC UNIVERSITY OF IRELAND,
AND PRIEST OF THE ORATORY OF ST. PHILIP NERI.

"ATTINGIT SAPIENTIA A FINE USQUE AD FINEM FORTITER, ET DISPONIT OMNIA
SUAVITER".

DUBLIN:
JAMES DUFFY, 7 WELLINGTON QUAY,
PUBLISHER TO HIS GRACE THE CATHOLIC ARCHBISHOP OF DUBLIN.
1852.

A17b

A

Books, Broadsides, Collections, Pamphlets, and Postscripts

A1a Apologia pro vita sua: being a reply to a pamphlet entitled "What, then, does Dr. Newman mean?" London: Longman, Green, Longman, Roberts, and Green, 1864.

In eight separate pamphlets:

Part I: Mr. Kingsley's method of disputation. pp. 1-25.
Part II: True mode of meeting Mr. Kingsley. pp. 29-51.
Part III: History of my religious opinions. pp. 55-100.
Part IV: History of my religious opinions. pp. 103-75.
Part V: History of my religious opinions. pp. 179-253.
Part VI: History of my religious opinions. pp. 257-369.
Part VII: General answer to Mr. Kingsley. pp. 373-430.
Appendix: Answer in detail to Mr. Kingsley's accusations. pp. 3-127.

A1b Apologia pro vita sua: being a reply to a pamphlet entitled "What, then, does Dr. Newman mean?" London: Longman, Green, Longman, Roberts, and Green, 1864.

iv, 430; 127 pp. (appendix).

This is the bound edition of the pamphlets with correction of minor errors. The appendix is separately paged and includes the eighth pamphlet, "Answer in detail to Mr. Kingsley's accusations"; notes quoting the Latin, French, and Italian originals of passages translated in the preceding section; a list of N's works; and a postscript giving Bishop Ullathorne's testimonial letter.

This work was next published in a revised edition with a change in title to *History of my religious opinions*. See **A32a**.

A1c Apologia pro vita sua: being a reply to a pamphlet entitled "What, then, does Dr. Newman mean?" New York: D. Appleton and Company, 1865.

393 pp.

Contents are the same as English first edition except the postscript giving letter of Ullathorne is omitted, and there is added "Mr. Kingsley and Dr. Newman: A correspondence on the question whether Dr. Newman teaches that truth is no virtue?"

A1d Apologia pro vita sua: being a reply to a pamphlet entitled "What, then, does Dr. Newman mean?" Third edition. New York: D. Appleton and Co., 1865.
393 pp.
New impression of **A1c.**

A1e Apologia pro vita sua: being a reply to a pamphlet entitled "What, then, does Dr. Newman mean?" Fourth edition. New York: D. Appleton and Company, 1865.
393 pp.
New impression of **A1c.**

A1f Apologia pro vita sua: being a reply to a pamphlet entitled "What, then, does Dr. Newman mean?" Fifth edition. New York: The Catholic Publication House, [n.d.].
393 pp.
New impression of **A1c.**

A1g Apologia pro vita sua: being a history of his religious opinions. New edition. London: Longmans, Green, Reader, and Dyer, 1873.
xxiv, 388 pp.
With this impression N reverted to the original title *Apologia pro vita sua*, but with the subtitle *Being a history of his religious opinions.* See **A32a,b,c** for previous edition and impressions.

A1h Apologia pro vita sua: being a history of his religious opinions. New edition. London: Longmans, Green, Reader, and Dyer, 1875.
xxiv, 388 pp.
New impression.

A1i   Apologia pro vita sua: being a history of his religious opinions. London: Longmans, Green, Reader, and Dyer, 1876.
xxiv, 388 pp.
New impression.

A1j   Apologia pro vita sua: being a history of his religious opinions. London: Longmans, Green, Reader, and Dyer, 1878.
xxiv, 395 pp.
Seven pages of notes added at the end, pp. 389-95.

A1k   Apologia pro vita sua: being a history of his religious opinions. London: Longmans, Green, Reader, and Dyer, 1879.
xxiv, 395 pp.
New impression.

A1l   Apologia pro vita sua: being a history of his religious opinions. London: Longmans, Green, Reader, and Dyer, 1881.
xxviii, 395 pp.
Extracts from the first edition, Part I, pp. 3, 20-25, added
to Preface, pp. xii-xv.

A1m   Apologia pro vita sua: being a history of his religious opinions. Longmans, Green, Reader, and Dyer, 1882.
xxviii, 395 pp.
New impression.

A1n   Apologia pro vita sua: being a history of his religious opinions. London: Longmans, Green, Reader, and Dyer, 1883.
xxviii, 395 pp.
New impression.

A1o   Apologia pro vita sua: being a history of his religious opinions. London: Longmans, Green, and Co., 1885.
xxviii, 395 pp.
New impression.

A1p   Apologia pro vita sua: being a history of his religious opinions. London: Longmans, Green, and Co., 1886.
xxviii, 395 pp.
New impression.

A1q   Apologia pro vita sua: being a history of his religious opin-

ions. London: Longmans, Green, and Co., 1887.
xxviii, 395 pp.
New impression.

A1r Apologia pro vita sua: being a history of his religious opinions. London and New York: Longmans, Green, and Co., 1888.
xxviii, 395 pp.
New impression.

A1s Apologia pro vita sua: being a history of his religious opinions. London and New York: Longmans, Green, and Co., 1889.
xxviii, 395 pp.
New impression.

A1t Apologia pro vita sua. New edition. London and New York: Longmans, Green, and Co., 1890.
xxviii, 395 pp.

A2a The Arians of the fourth century, their doctrine, temper and conduct, chiefly as exhibited in the Councils of the Church, between A.D. 325, and A.D. 381. London: Printed for J. G. & F. Rivington, 1833.
xi, 425 pp.
Copy at B.O. with corrections in N's hand.

A2b The Arians of the fourth century, their doctrine, temper and conduct, chiefly as exhibited in the Councils of the Church, between A.D. 325, and A.D. 381. Second edition (literally reprinted from the first edition). Preface by G. H. Forbes. London: E. Lumley, 1854.
x, 230 pp.
Copy at B.O. with corrections in N's hand.

A2c The Arians of the fourth century. London: Printed for private circulation only, 1871.
xix, 478 pp.
Fifty copies printed for private circulation. This is the same as **A2d**, but it is not clear which appeared first.

A2d The Arians of the fourth century. Third edition. London: E. Lumley, 1871.
xix, 478 pp.

Same as **A2c**. New edition. Advertisement to this edition mentions literary changes and additions to footnotes. Appendix added. Table of Contents and Chronological Table enlarged. Two sentences on Catholic Church put at end of appendix.

A2e The Arians of the fourth century. Fourth edition. London: Basil Montagu Pickering, 1876.

xix, 474 pp. and page of errata.

N made an addition to note V, at the end, pp. 464-68. Copy at B.O. with corrections in N's hand.

A2f The Arians of the fourth century. Fifth edition. London: Burns & Oates, Limited; New York: Catholic Publication Society Co., [1882]. [On spine: Pickering.]

xix, 474 pp.

A2g The Arians of the fourth century. Fifth edition. London and New York: Longmans, Green, and Co., 1888.

xix, 474 pp.

A2h The Arians of the fourth century. Sixth edition. London and New York: Longmans, Green, and Co., 1890.

xix, 474 pp.

A2i The Arians of the fourth century. Seventh edition. London and New York: Longmans, Green, and Co., 1890.

xix, 474 pp.

A3a Callista, a sketch of the third century. [Anon.] London: Burns and Lambert; Cologne: J. P. Bachem. [Title page 2:] Callista, a sketch of the third century. Poem by DeVere. London: Burns and Lambert; Cologne: J. P. Bachem, 1856.

iv, 296 pp. and frontispiece; advertisement, P.S., and Erratum running on.

Copy at B.O. inscribed: "John H. Newman, May, 1856" and "To J. F. Lynch with the very kind regards of the author. April 23, 1873."

Callista contains four poems: "Juba's song" (The little black moor is the mate for me); "Callista's song" (I wander by that river's brink); "Heathen Greece (A song)" (Where are the islands of the blest?); "A martyr convert" (The number of Thine own complete). The last two were reprinted in *V. V.* See **A97a.**

A3b Callista, a sketch of the third century. [Anon.] London: Burns and Lambert; Cologne: J. P. Bachem, 1856.
iv, 296 pp.
First edition sheets with advertisements and postscripts appearing on different pages, new and uncorrected impression and imprint on verso of title page: London: Gilbert and Rivington, Printers.

A3c Callista, a sketch of the third century. New York, Boston, etc.: D. & J. Sadlier & Company, [1856].
iv, 296 pp.

A3d Callista, a sketch of the third century. [Anon., but dedication signed: J.H.N.] London: Burns, Oates, & Co., [n.d.].
iv, 296 pp.
No address of publisher. Imprint, p. 296: London: Levey and Co., Printers, Great New Street, Fetter Lane, E.C.

A3e Callista, a sketch of the third century. [Anon., but dedication signed: J.H.N.] London: Burns, Oates, & Co., [n.d.].
[iv], 296 pp.
Copy carries dedication to H.W.W. on different page than in **A3d.** Also address of publisher given: 17 Portman Street and 63 Paternoster Row. Imprint, p. 296: Printed by John Levey, West Harding Street.

A3f Callista, a sketch of the third century. By John Henry Newman of the Oratory. Copyright edition. Leipzig: Bernhard Tauchnitz, 1869.
[iii], 334 pp.
New edition.

A3g Callista: a sketch of the third century. London: Burns, Oates, & Co., Basil Montagu Pickering, 1873.
x, 382 pp.
New edition.

A3h Callista, a sketch of the third century. London: Burns, Oates, & Co., Basil Montagu Pickering, 1876.

   x, 382 pp.

A3i Callista, a sketch of the third century. London: Burns and Oates, Pickering, 1881.

   xii, 382 pp.

   New edition. Another postscript added.

   Copy at B.O. with the following pasted in back in N's hand: "Some of the works I consulted for the accounts of the mass in Callista,/Marcelli Africa Vol. 2 p. 90/Assemann's Cod. t 4/Leslie Missal, Mozarat, p xl/Muratori Liturg. Rom. pp 14. 82, 3 241 etc. etc./Krazen de Liturgiis."

A3j Callista: a sketch of the third century. London: Burns and Oates; New York: Catholic Publication Society Co., 1885.

   xii, 382 pp.

   New and corrected edition.

   Copy at B.O. with corrections in N's hand.

A3k Callista, a tale of the third century. New edition. London and New York: Longmans, Green, and Co., 1889.

   xii, 382 pp.

A3l Callista, a tale of the third century. New edition. London: and New York: Longmans, Green, and Co., 1890.

   xii, 382 pp.

A4a Catholic University. The rector's report to their lordships the archbishops and bishops of Ireland for the year 1854–1855. [Signed at the end: John H. Newman.] Dublin: J. F. Fowler Printer, 1855.

   53 pp.

   Later published in *Campaign*, pp. 3-56. See **D11**.

A5a Catholic University. The rector's report to their lordships the archbishops and bishops of Ireland. For the year 1855–1856. [Signed at the end: John H. Newman.] Dublin: Printed by John F. Fowler, 1856.

   19 pp.; appendix, pp. i-lxx.

Later published in *Campaign*, pp. 57-73; appendix, pp. 75-167. See **D11**.

A6a Catholic University. The rector's report . . . for the year 1856–1857. [Signed, p. 18: John H. Newman.] Dublin: Printed by John F. Fowler, 1858.

18 pp.; appendix, pp. 19-35.

Later published in *Campaign*, pp. 169-84; appendix, pp. 185-208. See **D11**.

A7a Certain difficulties felt by Anglicans in Catholic teaching considered: In twelve lectures addressed to the party of the religious movement of 1833 [on spine: Difficulties of Anglicans and one asterisk]. London: Burns, Oates, & Co., 1876.

xvi, 350 pp.

Originally published as *Lectures on certain difficulties felt by Anglicans in submitting to the Catholic Church*, 1850. See **A37a-e**. Then as *Difficulties felt by Anglicans*, fourth edition, [1872]. See **A15a**. The pages of the latter through p. 350 are bound with a new title page. Letter addressed to Rev. E. B. Pusey is dropped, being transferred to Pickering edition. See next entry.

Later published as *Certain diff.*, I. See **A7c**.

A7b Certain difficulties felt by Anglicans in Catholic teaching considered: In a letter to the Rev. E. B. Pusey, D.D., on occasion of his Eirenicon of 1864; and in a letter to the duke of Norfolk, on occasion of Mr. Gladstone's Expostulation of 1874 [on spine: Difficulties of Anglicans and two asterisks]. London: Basil Montagu Pickering, 1876.

378 pp.

Letter to Pusey previously published separately. See **A44a-d**. Then in Difficulties felt by Anglicans, fourth edition, [1872]. See **A15a**.

Letter to duke of Norfolk previously published separately. See **A42a-f**.

A7b is next published as *Certain diff.*, II. See **A7d**.

A7c Certain difficulties felt by Anglicans in Catholic teaching considered: 1. In twelve lectures addressed to the party of the religious movement of 1833 [on spine: Difficulties of Anglicans and one asterisk]. Vol. I. Fifth edition. London: Burns and Oates, 1879.

xiv (2), 400 pp.
New edition.

A7d Certain difficulties felt by Anglicans in Catholic teaching considered: In a letter addressed to the Rev. E. B. Pusey, D.D., on occasion of his Eirenicon of 1864; and in a letter addressed to the duke of Norfolk, on occasion of Mr. Gladstone's Expostulation of 1874. Vol. II. London: B. M. Pickering, [1883 or 1884].

That this was reprinted in late 1883 or early 1884 is clear from the correspondence, but no copy was found.

A7e Certain difficulties felt by Anglicans in Catholic teaching considered: 1. In twelve lectures addressed to the party of the religious movement of 1833. Vol. I. London: Longmans, Green, and Co., 1885.

xvi, 400 pp.

A7f Certain difficulties felt by Anglicans in Catholic teaching considered: In a letter addressed to the Rev. E. B. Pusey, D.D., on occasion of his Eirenicon of 1864; and in a letter addressed to the duke of Norfolk, on occasion of Mr. Gladstone's Expostulation of 1874. Vol. II. London: Longmans, Green, and Co., 1885.

[ii], 378 pp.

A7g Certain difficulties felt by Anglicans. . . . 2 vols. London and New York: Longmans, Green, and Co., 1888.

xvi, 400 pp.; [ii], 378 pp.

A8a Characteristics from the writings of John Henry Newman, being selections personal, historical, philosophical, and religious, from his various works. Arranged by William Samuel Lilly of the Inner Temple, Barrister-at-Law, with the author's approval. London: Henry S. King & Co., 1874.

xvi, 447 pp.

A8b Characteristics from the writings of John Henry Newman, being selections personal, historical, philosophical, and religious, from his various works. Arranged by William Samuel Lilly of the Inner Temple, Barrister-at-Law, with the author's approval. London: Henry S. King, 1875.

    xvi, 477 pp.

A8c Characteristics from the writings of John Henry Newman, being selections personal, historical, and religious, from his various works, arranged by William Samuel Lilly of the Inner Temple, Barrister-at-Law. Second edition. New York: Scribner, Welford & Armstrong, 1875.

    xvi, 447 pp.

A8d Characteristics from the writings of John Henry Newman, being selections personal, historical, and religious, from his various works, arranged by William Samuel Lilly of the Inner Temple, Barrister-at-Law. Third edition. London: Henry S. King & Co., 1876.

    xvi, 447 pp.

A8e Characteristics from the writings of John Henry Newman, being selections personal, historical, and religious, from his various works, arranged by William Samuel Lilly of the Inner Temple, Barrister-at-Law. New York: D. & J. Sadlier & Co., 1878.

    353 pp.

A8f Characteristics from the writings of John Henry Newman, being selections personal, historical, and religious, from his various works, arranged by William Samuel Lilly of the Inner Temple, Barrister-at-Law. Fifth edition. London: C. Kegan Paul & Co., 1880.

    xvi, 447 pp.

A8g Characteristics from the writings of John Henry Newman, being selections personal, historical, and religious, from his various works, arranged by William Samuel Lilly of the Inner Temple, Barrister-at-Law. New York, Montreal: D. & J. Sadlier & Co., 1880.

    353 pp.

A8h Characteristics from the writings of John Henry Newman, being selections personal, historical, and religious, from his various works, arranged by William Samuel Lilly of the Inner Temple, Barrister-at-Law. New York, Montreal: D. & J. Sadlier & Co., 1881.

353 pp.

A8i Characteristics from the writings of John Henry Newman, being selections personal, historical, and religious, from his various works, arranged by William Samuel Lilly of the Inner Temple, Barrister-at-Law. Sixth edition. London: Kegan Paul, Trench & Co., 1882.

xvi, 447 pp.

A8j Characteristics from the writings of John Henry Newman, being selections personal, historical, and religious, from his various works, arranged by William Samuel Lilly of the Inner Temple, Barrister-at-Law. New York: D. & J. Sadlier & Co., 1884.

353 pp.

A8k Characteristics from the writings of John Henry Newman, being selections personal, historical, and religious, from his various works, arranged by William Samuel Lilly of the Inner Temple, Barrister-at-Law. New York & Montreal: D. & J. Sadlier & Co., 1885.

353 pp.

A8l Characteristics from the writings of John Henry Newman, being selections personal, historical, and religious, from his various works, arranged by William Samuel Lilly of the Inner Temple, Barrister-at-Law. Eighth edition. London: Kegan Paul, Trench & Co., 1888.

xvi, 447 pp.

A8m Characteristics from the writings of John Henry Newman, being selections personal, historical, and religious, from his various works, arranged by William Samuel Lilly of the Inner Temple, Barrister-at-Law. New York & Montreal: D. & J. Sadlier & Co., 1888.

353 pp.

A9a Christ upon the waters. A sermon preached in substance at St. Chad's, Birmingham on Sunday, October 27, 1850, on occasion of establishment of the Catholic hierarchy in this country. Published by the desire of the bishop [Ullathorne]. Birmingham: M. Maher; London: Burns and Lambert, [1850].
36 pp.

A9b Christ upon the waters. A sermon preached in substance at St. Chad's, Birmingham on Sunday, October 27, 1850, on occasion of establishment of the Catholic hierarchy in this country. Published by the desire of the bishop [Ullathorne]. Second edition. Birmingham: M. Maher; London: Burns and Lambert, [n.d.].
36 pp.

A9c Christ upon the waters. A sermon preached in substance at St. Chad's, Birmingham on Sunday, October 27, 1850, on occasion of establishment of the Catholic hierarchy in this country. Published by the desire of the bishop [Ullathorne]. Third edition. Birmingham: M. Maher; London: Burns and Lambert, [n.d.].
36 pp.

A9d Christ upon the waters. A sermon preached in substance at St. Chad's, Birmingham on Sunday, October 27, 1850, on occasion of establishment of the Catholic hierarchy in this country. Published by the desire of the bishop [Ullathorne]. Fourth edition. Birmingham: M. Maher; London: Burns & Lambert, 1852.
36 pp.
Later published in O.S. See **A84a**.

A10a The Church of the Fathers. [Anon.] London: Printed for J. G. F. & J. Rivington, 1840.
xii, 420 pp.
Originally published as "Letters on the Church of the Fathers" in the *British Magazine*, IV (Oct. 1833), 421, to XI (May 1837), 522. See **B3d**.
Contents:
   I   Ambrose and Justina

II   Ambrose and Valentinian
III   The martyrs Gervasius and Protasius
IV   The penitence of Theodosius
V   Basil the Great
VI   Trials of Basil
VII   Labours of Basil
VIII   Basil and Gregory
IX   Rise and fall of Gregory
X   Vincentius of Lerins
XI   Apollinaris
XII   Augustine and the Vandals
XIII   Conversion of Augustine
XIV   Demetrias
XV   Jovinian and his companions
XVI   Canons of the Apostles
XVII   Canons of the Apostles
XVIII   Antony in conflict
XIX   Antony in calm
XX   Martin, the Apostle of Gaul
XXI   Martin and Priscillian

A10b   The Church of the Fathers. [Anon.] Second edition. London: Printed for J. G. F. and J. Rivington, 1842.
    xii, 420 pp.
    Last paragraph of advertisement of first edition omitted. Correction on p. 143.

A10c   The Church of the Fathers. [N's name on title page.] A new edition. Dublin: James Duffy, 1857.
    xi, 362 pp.
    New edition. Quotation on title page put in Latin. New dedication. New advertisement replaces old one. Introduction added. Chs. I, II, III, IV, X, XV, XVI, XVII of first and second editions omitted; XX and XXI are abridged and reduced to one. Order of chapters changed. The omissions from this edition, with the exception of the chapter "The penitence of Theodosius," were later published in "Primitive Christianity," *H.S.*, I. See **A31a,c,k**.

Copy at B.O. with corrections in N's hand.

Contents:

    I Basil the Great

    II Trials of Basil

    III Labours of Basil

    IV Basil and Gregory

    V Rise and fall of Gregory

    VI Apollinaris

    VII Antony in conflict

    VIII Antony in calm

    IX Augustine and the Vandals

    X Conversion of Augustine

    XI Demetrias

    XII Martin, the Apostle of Gaul

A10d The Church of the Fathers. Fourth edition. London: Burns, Oates, and Company, 1868.

xiv, 361 pp.

Restored dedication of 1840, retaining dedication of 1857. New advertisement added to previous advertisements. Literary corrections in advertisement to first and second editions and introduction.

Later published in *H.S.*, II. See **A31a,d,l**. Chapter on Apollinaris was put into "Primitive Christianity," *H.S.*, I. See **A31a,c,k**.

A11a The Church visible and invisible [from 3rd vol. of Parochial Sermons by Rev. J. H. Newman. Second edition. London: Rivingtons] [*sic*] with an appendix. London: James Burns, 1840.

24 pp.

See **A64b, A69a**.

A12a A correspondence between the Rev. J. H. Newman, D.D., and the bishop of Norwich [Samuel Hinds] on the credibility of miracles. Extracted from the *Morning Chronicle*. Birmingham: M. Freeman, later Lander, Powell, and Co., 1851.

8 pp.

Originally published in the *Morning Chronicle*, 21 Oct. 1851. See **B13a**. Later published as note in 1872 and subsequent editions of *Prepos*. See **A40e**.

A13a Criticisms urged against certain Catholic doctrines: by
J. H. N. [n.p., n.d.].

96 pp.

Contents:

Head I. Article "On the inspiration of scripture," *The
Nineteenth Century*, XV (Feb. 1884), 185-99. See
B14a.

Head II. Postscript to the above: What is of obligation
for a Catholic to believe concerning the inspiration of
the canonical scriptures, being a postscript. . . ." See
A100a, A59a.

Head III. Reprint of *The development of religious
error*. See **A14a.**

Later printed as *E.C.P.* and *S.E.* See **A28a, A87a.**

A14a The development of religious error by John Henry Cardinal
Newman. From "The Contemporary Review" of October, 1885.
London: Burns and Oates, 1886.

39 pp. The postscript appendix, pp. 25-39, was added to the
original article. See **B9a.**

Later printed as *On a criticism urged against a Catholic
doctrine*, 1889. See **A58a.** Also as Head III in *Criticisms
urged against certain Catholic doctrines*. See **A13a.** Next in
E.C.P. See **A28a.** Finally as Essay III in *S.E.* See **A87a.**

A15a Difficulties felt by Anglicans in Catholic teaching considered: I. In twelve lectures addressed to the party of the
religious movement of 1833. II. In a letter addressed to the
Rev. E. B. Pusey, D.D., on occasion of his Eirenicon of 1864.
Fourth edition. London: Burns, Oates & Co., [1872].

xvi, 496 pp.

Previously published separately as *Lectures on certain difficulties* and *A letter addressed to the Rev. E. B. Pusey*. See
A37a-e and **A44a-d.**

Copy at B.O. with revisions of N and II torn out. "Certain"
is inserted before "Difficulties." Corrections enumerated on
flyleaf opposite title page. Postscript in N's hand after Preface: "*Postscript*—187. Lord Macaulay writes in 1850 [*vid.
Life*, ch. XII, vol. 2. p. 286]. 'Read Newman's Lectures . . .

One lecture is evidently directed against me, though not by name.' This is a mistake; I do not even suspect to which Lecture Lord M. refers. At that date, 1850, I had only read some of his Essays as they successively appeared in the Edinburgh Review. On the whole I recollect only three places in what I have written where I have referred to him, and then without mention of his name, in 1852, 1854 and 1871, viz. Idea of a University, pp. 118 and 301 and Essays, vol. II, pp. 84, 86.''

Since N wanted both *A letter to the duke of Norfolk* and *A letter to Pusey* in one volume, he arranged to have Pickering put out a volume in 1876 containing them both. This meant that Burns, Oates had to remove *A letter to Pusey* from all the copies of the above edition. Pickering removed all the pages containing *A letter to Pusey* from all his copies of Burns, Oates's *Difficulties* and wrote asking them to do the same. Since each volume could be bought separately, the two were not specifically labeled "Vol. I" and "Vol. II," but two asterisks were affixed to what later became vol. II of *Certain difficulties* and one was affixed to the volume put out by Burns, Oates which later became vol. I of *Certain difficulties.* Both companies issued the respective volumes in 1876 with the new title *Certain difficutlies.* See **A7a,b.**

A16a Discourses addressed to mixed congregations. London: Longman, Brown, Green, and Longmans, 1849.
vi (2), 402 pp.
Copy at B.O. with corrections in N's hand.

A16b Discourses addressed to mixed congregations. Second edition. London: Longman, Brown, Green, and Longmans, 1850.
vi (2), 402 pp.

A16c Discourses addressed to mixed congregations. Boston: Patrick Donahoe, 1853.
viii, 282 pp.
American edition.

A16d Discourses addressed to mixed congregations. Third edition. Dublin: James Duffy, Wellington Quay, and London, 22, Paternoster Row, 1862.

> vi (1), 442 pp.
> New edition.

A16e Discourses addressed to mixed congregations. Fourth edition. London: Burns, Oates, & Co., 1871.

> viii, 380 pp.
> New edition.
> Copy at B.O. inscribed: "John H. Newman Feby 14. 1871," with corrections in N's hand.

A16f Discourses addressed to mixed congregations. Fifth edition. London: Burns, Oates, & Co., 1876.

> viii, 380 pp.
> New edition.

A16g Discourses addressed to mixed congregations. Sixth edition. London: Burns & Oates, 1881.

> viii, 380 pp.
> New edition.

A16h Discourses addressed to mixed congregations. Seventh edition. London: Burns and Oates, Limited; New York: Catholic Publication Society Co., 1886.

> viii, 376 pp.
> New edition.

A16i Discourses addressed to mixed congregations. Seventh edition. London, etc.: Longmans, Green, and Co., 1891.

> viii, 376 pp.

A17a Discourses on university education, addressed to the Catholics of Dublin. Dublin: James Duffy, 1852.

> The individual discourses and appendix were published separately with the above title, name of publisher, and the number and title of the discourse on the cover.
> Two copies of Discourse V at B.O. with corrections in N's hand.
> Discourse I: Introductory. pp. [3]-33.

This was probably first published in the *Tablet*, XIII (May 15, 1852), 307-9. See **B18b**.

Discourse II: Theology a branch of knowledge. pp. 35-66.

Discourse III: Bearing of theology on other branches of knowledge. pp. 67-101.

Discourse IV: Bearing of other branches of knowledge on theology. pp. 103-34.

Discourse V: General knowledge viewed as one philosophy. pp. 135-66.

Discourse VI: Philosophical knowledge its own end. pp. 167-99.

Discourse VII: Philosophical knowledge viewed in relation to mental acquirements. pp. 201-40.

Discourse VIII: Philosophical knowledge viewed in relation to professional. pp. 241-87.

Discourse IX: Philosophical knowledge viewed in relation to religion. pp. 289-31.

Discourse X: Duties of the Church towards philosophy. pp. 333-67.

Appendix to Discourses . . . 1853. pp. [371]-449.

A17b Discourses on the scope and nature of university education. Addressed to the Catholics of Dublin. Dublin: James Duffy, 1852.

xxx, [1-3] 449 pp.

Individual discourses without separate title pages are bound together with a new reworded title page; dedication and preface, pp. xxx; contents and corrigenda, pp. [2]; and appendix.

Two copies at B.O. with corrections in N's hand.

Later published with omissions and revisions as *The scope and nature of university education*, 1859. See **A77a**. Then in the *Idea*, Part I. See **A33a**.

A18a Discussions and arguments on various subjects. London: Basil Montagu Pickering, 1872.

viii, 398 pp.

Copy at B.O. with corrections in N's hand.

Contents:

> I. How to accomplish it.
> Originally published as "Home thoughts abroad. No. II," *British Magazine*, IX (March 1836), 237-48; (April 1836), 357-69. See **B3c**.
> II. The patristical idea of Antichrist.
> Originally published as *Advent sermons on Antichrist*, tract 83. See **C80a**.
> III. Holy scripture in its relation to the Catholic Creed.
> Originally published as *Lectures on the scripture proof of the doctrines of the Church*, tract 85. See **C81a**.
> IV. The Tamworth reading room.
> Originally published in *The Times*, 5, 9, 10, 12, 20, 22, 26 Feb. 1841. See **B19a**. Then as a pamphlet, *The Tamworth reading room*. See **A89a**.
> V. Who's to blame?
> Originally published in *Catholic Standard*, 3, 10, 17, 24, 31 March and 7, 14, 21 April 1855. See **B5a**.
> VI. An internal argument for Christianity.
> Originally published as "Ecce Homo," *The Month*, IV (June 1866), 551-73. See **B12c**.

A18b Discussions and arguments on various subjects. Second edition. London: Basil Montagu Pickering, 1873.

> viii, 404 pp. Index added.

A18c Discussions and arguments on various subjects. Third edition. London: Pickering and Co., 1878.

> viii, 404 pp.
>
> New and corrected impression.
>
> Copy at B.O. inscribed by N: "John H. Newman / Novr 2. 1878 / p. 292." A revision listed on p. 292 was evidently not incorporated in subsequent editions.

A18d Discussions and arguments on various subjects. Fourth edition. London: Pickering and Co., 1882.

> viii, 404 pp.
>
> New impression.

A18e Discussions and arguments on various subjects. Fourth edition. London: Longmans, Green and Co., 1885.
viii, 404 pp.

A18f Discussions and arguments on various subjects. Fifth edition. London and New York: Longmans, Green, and Co., 1888.
viii, 404 pp.
New impression.

A18g Discussions and arguments on various subjects. Sixth editions London and New York: Longmans, Green, and Co., 1888.
viii, 404 pp.
New impression.

A18h Discussions and arguments on various subjects. Seventh edition. London and New York: Longmans, Green, and Co., 1890.
viii, 404 pp.
New impression.

A19a Dissertatiunculae quaedam critico-theologicae auctore Joanne H. Newman anglo. Romae: Typis S. Congregationis de propaganda Fide, 1847.
68 pp.
Contents:
  1. De quarta oratione S. Athanasii contra Arianos
  2. De ecthesi ephesina contra Paulum Samosatenum
  3. De vocibus πρὶν γεννηϑῆναι οὐκ ἦν Anathematismi Nicaeni
  4. De vocibus ἐξ ἑτέρας ὑποστάσεως ἤ οὐσίας Anathematismi Nicaeni
Later published in *T.T.* See **A90a**.

A20a Dr. John Henry Newman's reply to Mr. Gladstone's pamphlet. Toronto: H. S. Irving & Co., 1875.
87 pp.
Canadian edition of *A letter addressed to His Grace the duke of· Norfolk on occasion of Mr. Gladstone's recent expostulation*, without postscript. See **A42a**.

A21a The dream of Gerontius. [Dedication signed: J.H.N.] London: Burns and Oates, 1865.

55 pp.

Originally published in *The Month*, II (May 1865), 415-25, (June 1865), 532-44. See **B12a**.

A21b The dream of Gerontius. [Dedication signed: J.H.N.] London: Burns, Lambert, and Oates, 1866.

55 pp.

New impression.

A21c The dream of Gerontius. [Dedication signed: J.H.N.] London: Burns, Lambert, and Oates, 1869.

55 pp.

New impression.

A21d The dream of Gerontius. [Dedication signed: J.H.N.] Seventeenth edition. London: Burns and Oates, 1883.

55 pp.

New impression.

A21e The dream of Gerontius. [Dedication signed: J.H.N.] Eighteenth edition. London: Burns and Oates, 1884.

55 pp.

New impression.

A21f The dream of Gerontius. [Dedication signed: J.H.N.] Twentieth edition. London: Burns and Oates; New York: Catholic Publications Society, 1885.

55 pp.

New impression.

A21g The dream of Gerontius. [Dedication signed: J.H.N.] Twenty-first edition. London: Burns and Oates; New York: Catholic Publications Society, 1886.

55 pp.

New impression.

A21h The dream of Gerontius. [Dedication signed: J.H.N.] London: Burns and Oates, 1886.

60 pp.

New edition.

A21i The dream of Gerontius. [Dedication signed: J.H.N.] Twenty-third edition. London and New York: Longmans, Green, and Co., 1888.

> 60 pp.
> New impression.

A21j The dream of Gerontius. [Dedication signed: J.H.N.] Twenty-fourth edition. London and New York: Longmans, Green, and Co., 1888.

> 60 pp.
> New impression.

A21k The dream of Gerontius. [Dedication signed: J.H.N.] Twenty-fifth edition. London and New York: Longmans, Green, and Co., 1889.

> 60 pp.
> New impression.

A21l The dream of Gerontius. [Dedication signed: J.H.N.] Twenty-seventh edition. London, New York, and Bombay: Longmans, Green, and Co., 1890.

> 60 pp.
> New impression.

A22a Echoes from the Oratory. Selections from the poems of the Rev. John Henry Newman. New York: Anson D. F. Randolph & Company, 1864.

> 61 pp.

A22b Echoes from the Oratory. Selections from the poems of the Rev. John Newman. New York: A. D. F. Randolph & Co., 1884.

> 61 pp.

A23a Elucidations of Dr. Hampden's theological statements. [Anon.] Oxford: Printed by W. Baxter. Sold by J. H. Parker; and by Messrs. Rivington, London, 1836.

> 47 pp.

A24a An essay in aid of a grammar of assent. London: Burns, Oates, & Co., 1870.

    viii, 485 pp.

    Copy at B.O. with corrections in N's hand.

A24b An essay in aid of a grammar of assent. New York: The Catholic Publication Society, 1870.

    viii, 479 pp.

A24c An essay in aid of a grammar of assent. New York: Christian Press Association Publishing Company, [n.d.].

    viii, 479 pp.

A24d An essay in aid of a grammar of assent. Second edition. London: Burns, Oates, & Co., 1870.

    viii, 485 pp.

A24e An essay in aid of a grammar of assent. Third edition. London: Burns, Oates, & Co., 1870.

    viii, 485 pp.

A24f An essay in aid of a grammar of assent. Fourth edition. London: Burns, Oates, & Co., 1874.

    viii, 494 pp.

    Note I added.

A24g An essay in aid of a grammar of assent. Fifth edition. London: Burns & Oates, 1881.

    viii, 501 pp.

    Note II added.

    Copy at B.O. with annotation by N: "These corrections I cancel and made on the copy in my book shelf."

    Thirteen-line insertion pasted into p. 423.

A24h An essay in aid of a grammar of assent. Fifth edition. London: Burns & Oates, 1881.

    viii, 503 pp.

    Note III added, but dated: December, 1882.

A24i An essay in aid of a grammar of assent. Fifth edition. London: Longmans, Green and Co., 1885.

    viii, 503 pp.

A24j An essay in aid of a grammar of assent. Sixth edition. London: Longmans, Green and Co., 1887.
viii, 503 pp.

A24k An essay in aid of a grammar of assent. Seventh edition. London: Longmans, Green and Co., 1888.
viii, 503 pp.

A24l An essay in aid of a grammar of assent. Eighth edition. London and New York: Longmans, Green and Co., 1889.
viii, 503 pp.

A24m An essay in aid of a grammar of assent. New edition. London and New York: Longmans, Green and Co., 1891.
viii, 503 pp.

A25a An essay on the development of Christian doctrine. London: James Toovey, 1845.
xv, 453 pp.
Copy at B.O. with inscription: "John H. Newman, *1846.* This is the *philosophical* work of a writer who was *not a Catholic*, and did not pretend to be a *theologian*, addressed to those who were not *Catholics*."
Another copy at B.O. with corrections for the 1878 edition.

A25b An essay on the development of Christian doctrine. New York: D. Appleton & Co.; Philadelphia: Geo. S. Appleton; Cincinnati: Derby, Bradley & Co., [n.d.].
206 pp.
American edition.

A25c An essay on the development of Christian doctrine. Second edition. London: James Toovey, 1846.
xv, 453 pp.
Errors of first edition corrected. Introduction seems to have been reset.

A25d An essay on the development of Christian doctrine. New edition. London: Basil Montagu Pickering, 1878.
xvi, 443 pp.
New and completely revised edition. Preface added.

Copy at B.O. with corrections in N's hand and inscribed: "John H Newman Febr 23. 1878."

A25e An essay on the development of Christian doctrine. New edition. London: Pickering & Co., 1881.

xvi, 445 pp.

Copy at B.O. with corrections and additions in N's hand. "Fifth" written over "New"; "Longmans, Green" substituted for "Pickering" and "1888" for "1881."

A25f An essay on the development of Christian doctrine. New edition. London: Longmans, Green and Co., 1885.

xvi, 445 pp.

A25g An essay on the development of Christian doctrine. Fifth edition. London: Longmans, Green and Co., 1888.

xvi, 445 pp.

Copy at B.O. with insertions by N.

A25h An essay on the development of Christian doctrine. Sixth edition. London and New York: Longmans, Green, and Co., 1888.

xvi, 445 pp.

A25i An essay on the development of Christian doctrine. Sixth edition. London and New York: Longmans, Green, and Co., 1890.

xvi, 445 pp.

A25j An essay on the development of Christian doctrine. Seventh edition. London and New York: Longmans, Green, and Co., 1890.

xvi, 445 pp.

A26a An essay on the miracles recorded in the ecclesiastical history of the early ages. Oxford: John Henry Parker; London: J. G. and F. Rivington, 1843.

ccxv (1) pp.

Originally published as an introduction to Fleury's *Ecclesiastical history*. See **C17a**.

Copy at B.O. with corrections in N's hand.

Later published in *Mir.* See **A92a**.

A27a Essays critical and historical. 2 vols. London: Basil Montagu Pickering, 1871.

>   ix, 424 pp.; (1) 455 pp.

>   Copy at B.O. with corrections in N's hand.

>   Contents:

>   Vol. I:

>   I. Poetry with reference to Aristotle's *Poetics*. Note on Essay I.

>   Essay originally published as "Greek tragedy—poetry" in *London Review* I (1828), 153-71. See **B1l**.

>   II. The introduction of rationalistic principles into revealed religion. Note on Essay II.

>   Essay originally published as *On the introduction of rationalistic principles into religion*, tract 73. See **C74a**.

>   III. The fall of La Mennais. Note on Essay III.

>   Essay originally published as *"Affairs of Rome"* in *The British Critic*, XXI (Oct. 1837), 261-83. See **B2f**.

>   IV. Palmer's view of faith and unity. Note on Essay IV.

>   Essay originally published as "Palmer's *Treatise on the Church of Christ*," in *The British Critic*, XXIV (Oct. 1838), 347-72. See **B2j**.

>   V. The theology of St. Ignatius. Note on Essay V.

>   Essay originally published as "Jacobson's *Apostolical Fathers—Ignatius*," in *The British Critic*, XXV (Jan. 1839), 49-76. See **B2k**.

>   VI. Prospects of the Anglican Church. Note on Essay VI.

>   Essay originally published as *"State of religious parties"* in *The British Critic*, XXV (April 1839), 396-426. See **B2m**.

>   VII. The Anglo-American Church. Note on Essay VII.

>   Essay originally published as *"The American Church"* in *The British Critic*, XXVI (Oct. 1839), 281-343. See **B2n**.

>   VIII. Selina, countess of Huntingdon.

>   Originally published as *"Memoir of the countess of Huntingdon*," in *The British Critic*, XXVIII (Oct. 1840), 263-95. See **B2s**.

Vol. II:

IX. The catholicity of the Anglican Church. Note on Essay IX.

Essay originally published as *"Catholicity of the English Church,"* in *The British Critic*, XXVII (Jan. 1840), 40-88. See **B2q**.

X. The Protestant idea of Antichrist.

Originally published as "Todd's *Discourses on the prophecies relating to Antichrist,"* in *The British Critic*, XXVIII (Oct. 1840), 391-440. See **B2t**.

XI. Milman's view of Christianity.

Originally published as "Milman's *History of Christianity,"* in *The British Critic*, XXIX (Jan. 1841), 71-114. See **B2u**.

XII. The reformation of the eleventh century. Note on Essay XII.

Essay originally published as "Bowden's *Life of Gregory VII—Reformation of the eleventh century,"* in *The British Critic*, XXIX (April 1841), 280-331. See **B2v**.

XIII. Private judgment.

Originally published as *"Private judgment,"* in *The British Critic*, XXX (July 1841), 100-134. See **B2w**.

XIV. John Davison.

Originally published as *"Works of the late Rev. J. Davison,"* in *The British Critic*, XXXI (April 1842), 367-401. See **B2y**.

XV. John Keble.

Originally published as "Lyra innocentium by the author of the Christian year," *The Dublin Review*, XX (June 1846), 434-61. See **B10b**.

A27b Essays critical and historical. Second edition. 2 vols. London: B. M. Pickering, 1872.

ix, 424 pp; (1) 455 pp.

New impression.

A27c Essays critical and historical. Third edition. 2 vols. London: Basil Montagu Pickering, 1873.

ix, 424 pp.; (1) 463 pp.

New impression. Index added at the end.

A27d Essays critical and historical. Fourth edition. 2 vols. London: Basil Montagu Pickering, 1877.

ix, 424 pp.; (1) 463 pp.

New impression.

A27e Essays critical and historical. Fifth edition. 2 vols. London: Pickering and Co., 1881.

ix (1), 425 pp.; (1) 463 pp.

Copy at B.O. with corrections in N's hand and note: "NB correct this advertisement by the portion quoted of it in beginning of *Via Media*, ed. 1882."

Note on the text of the Epistles of St. Ignatius in vol. 1 dropped from this edition and put in *T.T.* (beginning with second edition). See **A90b**.

"Apostolical tradition," originally published as *"The Brothers' controversy—apostolical tradition,"* British Critic, XIX (July 1836), 166-99, was added to this edition as Essay III in vol. 1. See **B2b**. The numbering of all the subsequent essays in both volumes is changed. New index.

A27f Essays critical and historical. Fifth edition. 2 vols. London: Longmans, Green, and Co., 1885.

ix (1), 425 pp.; (1) 463 pp.

A27g Essays critical and historical. Sixth edition. 2 vols. London: Longmans, Green and Co., 1885.

ix (1), 425 pp.; (1) 463 pp.

New and corrected impression. In vol. 1, corrections on pp. vi, 414, 425, and note added at the end of Essay IX, p. 425. In vol. 2, corrections on pp. 76, 326, and note omitted on p. 455.

A27h Essays critical and historical. Seventh edition. 2 vols. London and New York: Longmans, Green and Co., 1887.

ix (1), 425 pp.; (1) 463 pp.

New impression.

A27i Essays critical and historical. Eighth edition. 2 vols. London and New York: Longmans, Green and Co., 1888.

ix (1), 425 pp.; (1) 463 pp.

New impression.

A27j Essays critical and historical. Ninth edition. 2 vols. London and New York: Longmans, Green and Co., 1890.

ix (1), 425 pp.; (1) 463 pp.

New impression.

A27k Essays critical and historical. Tenth edition. 2 vols. London and New York: Longmans, Green and Co., 1890.

ix (1), 425 pp.; (1) 463 pp.

New impression.

A28a Essays on controversial points variously illustrated: by J.H.N. [n.p., n.d.].

96 pp.

The same as *Criticisms urged against certain Catholic doctrines*. See **A13a**. Both of these works seem to be preliminary versions of *S.E.* See **A87a**.

A29a Fifteen sermons preached before the University of Oxford, between A.D. 1826 and 1843. Third edition. London, etc.: Rivingtons, 1872.

xxiii, 351 pp.

New and revised edition. Dedication, preface, and notes added.

Originally published as *Sermons, chiefly on the theory of religious belief, preached before the University of Oxford*, 1843. See **A83a,b**.

Copy at B.O. inscribed "John H Newman / Jany 11. 1872" with corrections in N's hand.

A29b Fifteen sermons preached before the University of Oxford, between A.D. 1826 and 1843. Third edition. New York: Scribner, Welford & Co., 1872.

xxiii, 351 pp.

A29c Fifteen sermons preached before the University of Oxford, between A.D. 1826 and 1843. New edition. London: Rivingtons, 1880.

xxiii, 351 pp.

A29d Fifteen sermons preached before the University of Oxford, between A.D. 1826 and 1843. New edition. London: Rivingtons, 1884.

xxiii, 351 pp.

A29e Fifteen sermons preached before the University of Oxford, between A.D. 1826 and 1843. New edition. London: Rivingtons, 1887.

xxiii, 351 pp.

A29f Fifteen sermons preached before the University of Oxford, between A.D. 1826 and 1843. [On spine: J. H. Newman's Oxford University sermons.] New edition. London: Rivingtons, 1890.

xxiii, 351 pp.

A30a Five letters on Church reform, addressed to the "Record." Published in that paper in 1833. [Signed: "A Churchman."] Privately re-printed, 1871.

22 pp.

Originally published as "Church reform," *The Record*, 28, 31 Oct. and 7, 11, 14 Nov. 1833. See **B17a-e**.

A31a Historical sketches, 3 vols.

Note: In 1872 N published the first of the three volumes. It contained "Rise and progress of universities," etc. The second, containing "The Turks in their relation to Europe," etc., was also published in 1872. The third volume, "The Church of the Fathers," etc., was published in 1873. These were advertised as first series, second series, and third series, respectively. Since N intended that in the completed set "Rise and progress of universities" should be vol. 3, "The Turks," vol. 1, and "The Church of the Fathers," vol. 2, the works were printed without any volume being named on the title page. The new title pages giving the volume numbers were issued with the third volume in order of publication and with a note to the binder: "To the Binder. The title pages given at the beginning of each volume of Historical Sketches are to be cancelled, and those here given are to be substituted, the Index being placed at the end of Volume III." These title pages were:

Historical sketches. Vol. I. The Turks. . . . London: Basil Montagu Pickering, 1873.

Historical sketches. Vol. II. The Church of the Fathers. . . . London: Basil Montagu Pickering, 1873.

Historical sketches. Vol. III. Rise and progress of universities. . . . London: Basil Montagu Pickering, 1873.

Index. [10 pages unnumbered.]

Unfortunately the binders who, Pickering wrote to N, "are more than usually stupid," did not always follow out instructions, and there are copies of "The Church of the Fathers," the third in order of publication, which have the new title pages for the three volumes and sometimes the note to the binder—all bound in with the index at the end. Consequently some copies of the early editions carry the original title pages; others, the substituted title pages.

Adding to the confusion of binders, booksellers, and buyers, Pickering placed two asterisks on the spine of "The Turks" and three on the spine of "The Church of the Fathers," and no asterisk, or later one, on the spine of "Rise and progress of universities." These asterisks do not correspond to the volume numbers but to the order of publication. Newman received so many complaints about this that he brought the matter to Pickering's attention in 1876, but the system was not abandoned until after Pickering's death in 1878, when Alexander D. Denny took over the firm. A circular was printed and sent to booksellers:

19 Piccadilly, London

In order to prevent confusion, we beg to inform you that Dr. Newman's "Historical Sketches" will appear in future as follows:

Vol. I.	(formerly **)	The Turks in their relation to Europe, etc.
Vol. II	(formerly ***)	The Church of the Fathers, etc.

Vol. III   (formerly *)   Rise and Progress of Universi-
                                           ties, etc.
The stars will be disused in future. We are,
                                      Your obedient servants,
                                      Pickering and Co.

A31b Historical sketches. Rise and progress of universities.
Northmen and Normans in England and Ireland. Medieval Oxford. Convocation of Canterbury. [On spine: J. H. Newman's
Historical sketches.] London: Basil Montagu Pickering, 1872.
   [iv] , 421 pp.
      Copy at B.O. with corrections in N's hand.
      Contents:
         I. Rise and progress of universities.
            Originally published in *Catholic University Gazette*
            and collected in *O.W.* See **B6** and **A57a,b**.
         II. Northmen and Normans in England and Ireland.
            Originally published as "The mission of the isles of
            the north," *The Rambler*, I, n.s. (May 1859), 1-22,
            (July 1859), 170-85. See **B16f**.
         III. Medieval Oxford.
            Originally published as *"Memorials of Oxford,"* The
            British Critic, XXIV (July 1838), 133-46. See **B2h**.
         IV. Convocation of Canterbury.
            Originally published as "The convocation of the prov-
            ince of Canterbury," *British Magazine*, VI (Nov.
            1834), 517-24, (Dec. 1834), 637-47; VII (Jan. 1835),
            33-41, (Feb. 1835), 145-54, (March 1835), 259-68.
            See **B3b**.

A31c Historical sketches. The Turks in their relation to Europe.
   Marcus Tullius Cicero. Apollonius of Tyana. Primitive Christianity. [On spine: J. H. Newman's Historical sketches and two
   asterisks.] London: Basil Montagu Pickering, 1872.
      xii (1), 446 pp.
      Copy at B.O. with corrections in N's hand.
      Contents:
         I. The Turks in their relation to Europe.

Originally published as *Lectures on the history of the Turks*. See **A38a**.

II. Marcus Tullius Cicero.

Originally published as "Marcus Tullius Cicero" in *Encyclopaedia metropolitana*, Third Division. See **C9b**.

III. Apollonius of Tyana.

Originally published as "The life of Apollonius of Tyanaeus" in *Encyclopaedia metropolitana*, Third Division. See **C9c**. Then separately. See **A49a**.

IV. Primitive Christianity.

Originally published in "Letters on the Church of the Fathers," *British Magazine*. See **B3d**. Then in *The Church of the Fathers* (1st and 2d eds.). See **A10a,b**.

A31d Historical sketches. The Church of the Fathers. St. John Chrysostom. Theodoret. Mission of St. Benedict. Benedictine schools. [On spine: J. H. Newman's Historical sketches and three asterisks.] London: Basil Montagu Pickering, 1873.

xiii (1), 487 pp.

Copy at B.O. with inscription: "John H / Newman, July 9, 1873" and corrections in N's hand.

Contents:

I. The Church of the Fathers.

Originally published as "Letters on the Church of the Fathers," in *The British Magazine*. See **B3d**. Then separately. See **A10a-d**.

II. The last years of St. John Chrysostom.

Originally published as "The ancient Saints," *The Rambler* I, n.s. (May 1859), 90-98; II (Nov. 1859), 41-62; III (July 1860), 189-203, (Sept. 1860), 338-57. See **B16b-e**.

III. Trials of Theodoret.

IV. The mission of St. Benedict.

Originally published as "The mission of the Benedictine order," *The Atlantis*, I (Jan. 1858), 1-49. See **B1a**.

V. The Benedictine schools.

Originally published as "The Benedictine centuries," *The Atlantis*, II (Jan. 1859), 1-43. See **B1c**.

A31e Historical sketches. The Turks in their relation to Europe. Marcus Tullius Cicero. Apollonius of Tyana. Primitive Christianity. Second edition. London: Basil Montagu Pickering, 1873.
xii (1), 446 pp.

A31f Historical sketches. The Turks in their relation to Europe. Marcus Tullius Cicero. Apollonius of Tyana. Primitive Christianity. Second edition. [Vol. I on spine.] London: Basil Montagu Pickering, 1873.
xii (1), 446 pp.

A31g Historical sketches. Rise and progress of universities. Northmen and Normans in England and Ireland. Medieval Oxford. Convocation of Canterbury. Second edition. London: Basil Montagu Pickering, 1873.
[iv], 421 pp.
New impression.

A31h Historical sketches. Rise and progress of universities. Northmen and Normans in England and Ireland. Medieval Oxford. Convocation of Canterbury. Third edition. [On spine: Historical sketches—Newman and one asterisk.] London: Basil Montagu Pickering, 1875.
[iv], 421 pp., plus index.
New impression.

A31i Historical sketches. The Turks in their relation to Europe. Marcus Tullius Cicero. Apollonius of Tyana. Primitive Christianity. Third edition. [On spine: J. H. Newman's Historical sketches and two asterisks.] London: Basil Montagu Pickering, 1876.
xii (1), 446 pp.
New impression.

A31j Historical sketches. The Church of the Fathers. St. John Chrysostom. Theodoret. Mission of St. Benedict. Benedictine schools. [On spine: J. H. Newman's Historical sketches and three asterisks.] London: Basil Montagu Pickering, 1876.

xiii (1), 487 pp., plus title pages for 3 vols. and index.
New impression.

A31k Historical sketches. Vol. I. The Turks in their relation to
Europe. Marcus Tullius Cicero. Apollonius of Tyana. Primitive
Christianity. London: Basil Montagu Pickering, 1876.

xii (1), 446 pp.

Copy at B.O. inscribed: "John Henry Newman, Nov.ʳ 2.
1878" with corrections in N's hand. On fly leaf: "p. 301, fr
1824 read 1826." This correction was made in Longmans'
edition 1886.

A31l Historical sketches. Vol. II. The Church of the Fathers.
St. John Chrysostom. Theodoret. Mission of St. Benedict. Benedictine schools. London: Basil Montagu Pickering, 1876.

xiii (1), 487 pp.

A31m Historical sketches. Vol. III. Rise and progress of univer-
sities. Northmen and Normans in England and Ireland. Medieval
Oxford. Convocation of Canterbury. London: Basil Montagu
Pickering, 1876.

[iv], 421 pp. plus 10 pages of index unnumbered.

A31n Historical sketches. Vol. I. The Turks in their relation to
Europe. Marcus Tullius Cicero. Apollonius of Tyana. Primitive
Christianity. Fourth edition. London: Pickering and Co., 1878.

xii (1), 446 pp.

New impression.

A31o Historical sketches. Vol. II. The Church of the Fathers.
St. John Chrysostom. Theodoret. Mission of St. Benedict. Benedictine schools. London: Pickering and Co., 1881.

xiii (1), 487 pp.

Copy at B.O. inscribed: "J. H. Newman. Has this volume
been revised?" Note by Fr. Neville: "The following corrections seem to have been made in the edition of 1884." Page
numbers listed.

A31p Historical sketches. Vol. III. Rise and progress of universities. Northmen and Normans in England and Ireland. Medieval

Oxford. Convocation of Canterbury. London: Pickering and Co., 1881.

[iv], 421 pp.

New impression.

Copy at B.O. with corrections in N's hand. "Longmans, Green and Co." written over "Pickering and Co." "1881" changed to "1888."

A31q Historical sketches. Vol. I. The Turks in their relation to Europe. Marcus Tullius Cicero. Apollonius of Tyana. Primitive Christianity. Fifth edition. London: Pickering and Co., 1882.

xii (1), 446 pp.

New and corrected impression.

A31r Historical sketches. Vol. II. The Church of the Fathers. St. John Chrysostom. Theodoret. Mission of St. Benedict. Benedictine schools. London: Pickering and Co., 1884.

xiii (1), 487 pp.

New impression.

A31s Historical sketches. Vol. III. Rise and progress of universities. Northmen and Normans in England and Ireland. Medieval Oxford. Convocation of Canterbury. London: Longmans, Green and Co., 1885.

[iv], 421 pp.

Probably not a new impression.

A31t Historical sketches. Vol. I. The Turks in their relation to Europe. Marcus Tullius Cicero. Apollonius of Tyana. Primitive Christianity. Sixth edition. London: Longmans, Green, and Co., 1886.

xii (1), 446 pp.

New impression.

A31u Historical sketches. Vol. I. The Turks in their relation to Europe. Marcus Tullius Cicero. Apollonius of Tyana. Primitive Christianity. Seventh edition. London and New York: Longmans, Green, and Co., 1888.

xii (1), 446 pp.

New impression.

A31v Historical sketches. Vol. I. The Turks in their relation to Europe. Marcus Tullius Cicero. Apollonius of Tyana. Primitive Christianity. Eighth edition. London and New York: Longmans, Green and Co., 1888.

> xii (1), 446 pp.
> New impression.

A31w Historical sketches. Vol. II. The Church of the Fathers. St. John Chrysostom. Theodoret. Mission of St. Benedict. Benedictine schools. London and New York: Longmans, Green and Co., 1888.

> xiii (1), 487 pp.
> New impression.

A31x Historical sketches. Vol. III. Rise and progress of universities. Northmen and Normans in England and Ireland. Medieval Oxford. Convocation of Canterbury. London and New York: Longmans, Green, and Co., 1888.

> [iv], 421 pp.
> New and corrected impression.

A31y Historical sketches. Vol. III. Rise and progress of universities. Northmen and Normans in England and Ireland. Medieval Oxford. Convocation of Canterbury. New edition. London and New York: Longmans, Green, and Co., 1889.

> [iv], 421 pp.

A32a History of my religious opinions. London: Longman, Green, Longman, Roberts, and Green, 1865.

> xxiv, 379 pp.
> New edition.
> Originally published as *Apologia pro vita sua* (1864). See **A1a,b**.
> A preface replaces the polemical Parts I and II of the first edition; a series of Notes numbered A to G recasts "Answer in detail to Mr. Kingsley's accusations," eliminating references to Kingsley; two new notes: A and B, "Liberalism" and "Series of Saints' lives of 1843–44," as well as a partially new one: D. "Ecclesiastical miracles." In section of "supple-

mental matter," a chronological list of the letters and papers quoted and letters of approbation . . . from clergy and laity are added.

A32b History of my religious opinions. New edition. London: Longmans, Green, Reader, and Dyer, 1869.
xxiv, 388 pp. "Additional Notes" added at the end.
Title page, publisher, and date listed as given by [C].

A32c History of my religious opinions. London: Longmans, Green, Reader, and Dyer, 1870.
xxiv, 388 pp.
Next published as *Apologia pro vita sua: being a history of his religious opinions*, 1873. See **A1g**.

A33a The idea of a university defined and illustrated I. in nine discourses addressed to the Catholics of Dublin II. in occasional lectures addressed to the members of the Catholic University. Third edition. London: Basil Montagu Pickering. 1873.
xxii, 527 pp.
Part I was originally published as *Discourses on university education*. See **A17a**. Then as *The scope and nature of university education*, 1859. See **A77a**. With this new and revised edition N reverted to the first edition text with some change in Discourses I and II. The latter two had been combined in the second edition. Discourse V not restored.
Part II was previously published as *Lectures and essays on university subjects*. See **A35a**.
Copy at B.O. inscribed: "John H. Newman / July 1873" with corrections in N's hand.

A33b The idea of a university defined and illustrated I. in nine discourses addressed to the Catholics of Dublin II. in occasional lectures addressed to the members of the Catholic University. Fourth edition. London: Basil Montagu Pickering, 1875.
xxii (1), 527 pp.
New impression.

A33c The idea of a university defined and illustrated I. in nine discourses addressed to the Catholics of Dublin II. in occasional lectures addressed to the members of the Catholic University. Fifth edition. London: B. M. Pickering, 1881.

 xxii (1), 527 pp.
 New impression.

A33d The idea of a university defined and illustrated I. in nine discourses addressed to the Catholics of Dublin II. in occasional lectures addressed to the members of the Catholic University. Fifth edition. Longmans, Green, and Co., 1885.

 xxii (1), 527 pp.

A33e The idea of a university defined and illustrated I. in nine discourses addressed to the Catholics of Dublin II. in occasional lectures addressed to the members of the Catholic University. Sixth edition. London: B. M. Pickering, 1886.

 xxii (1), 527 pp.
 New impression.

A33f The idea of a university defined and illustrated I. in nine discourses addressed to the Catholics of Dublin II. in occasional lectures addressed to the members of the Catholic University. Seventh edition. London: Longmans, Green, and Co., 1887.

 xxii (1), 527 pp.
 New impression.

A33g The idea of a university defined and illustrated I. in nine discourses addressed to the Catholics of Dublin II. in occasional lectures addressed to the members of the Catholic University. Eighth edition. London and New York: Longmans, Green, and Co., 1888.

 xxii (1), 527 pp.

A33h The idea of a university defined and illustrated I. in nine discourses addressed to the Catholics of Dublin II. in occasional lectures addressed to the members of the Catholic University. Ninth edition. London and New York: Longmans, Green, and Co., 1889.

 xxii (1), 527 pp.
 New impression.

A34a Lead, kindly light. Illustrated. Boston: Roberts Brothers, 1884.
> Not numbered. (16) ff.
> Originally published as "Faith" in "Lyra apostolica no. IX," *British Magazine*, V (Feb. 1, 1834), 153-56. See **B3j**. Later published as "Light in the darkness," in *Lyra apostolica*. See **C33a**. Then as "Grace of congruity" in *VRS*. See **A96a**. Lastly, as "The pillar of the cloud," in *V.V.* See **A97a**.

A34b Lead, kindly light. Boston: Roberts Brothers, 1884.
> 10 leaves.

A34c Lead, kindly light. Troy, N.Y.: Nims & Knight, 1887.
> (2) pp. (9) ff. Plates. Words only.

A35a Lectures and essays on university subjects. London: Longman, Brown, Green, Longman, and Roberts, 1859.
> vi (1), 387 pp.
> Later published as Part II of *Idea* with a slight change in the order of the chapters. See **A33a**.
> Contents:
>> I. Christianity and letters.
>> Originally published as "On the place held by the Faculty of Arts in the university course," *The Catholic University Gazette*, I (Nov. 16, 1854), 193-200. See **B6y**.
>> II. Literature.
>> Originally published as *The nature and characteristics of literature*, 1858. See **A56a**.
>> III. Catholic literature in the English tongue, 1854–58.
>> Sections 1, 2, and 3 were originally published as "On the formation of a Catholic literature in the English tongue," *The Catholic University Gazette*, I (Aug. 31, 1854), 105-9, (Sept. 7, 1854), 113-19. See **B6o,p**.
>> IV. Elementary studies.
>> Sections 1, 2, and part of 3 were originally published as "The examination at entrance," *The Catholic University Gazette*, I (June 1, 1854), 5-7; "The entrance examination a trial of accuracy," I (June 22, 1854), 25-32; "Specimens of youthful inaccuracy of mind,"

I (July 6, 1854), 41-47; "On Latin composition," I (Jan. 18, 1855), 294-96. See **B6b,e,g,ff.**
V. University preaching, 1855.
Originally published as "Letter of the rector to the Right Rev. D. Moriarity, D.D., bishop of Antigonia, coajutor-bishop of Kerry, on the subject of university preaching," *The Catholic University Gazette*, I (March 8, 1855), 394-400, and "Preaching with or without a book," I (April 5, 1855), 416-19. See **B6nn,oo.**
VI. Christianity and physical science.
Originally published as "On the general relations between theology and physical science," *The Catholic University Gazette*, II (Jan. 3, 1856), 2-14. See **B6uu.**
VII. Christianity and scientific investigation.
VIII. A form of infidelity of the day.
Originally published as "On the nascent infidelity of the day," *The Catholic University Gazette*, I (Dec. 21, 1854), 236-40, (Dec. 28, 1854), 243-48. See **B6dd.**
IX. Discipline of mind.
Originally published in part as "Public lectures of the university. [A letter] to the editor of the University Gazette," *The Catholic University Gazette*, I (April 5, 1855), 420-22. See **B6pp.**
X. Christianity and medical science.
Originally published as *Relations between medical science and theology*, 1858. See **A73a.**

A36a Lectures on Catholicism in England, delivered in the Corn Exchange, Birmingham. [Cheap edition.] Birmingham, 1851.
385 pp.
Cheap edition of *Lectures on the present position of Catholics in England*, 1851. See **A40a.** No dedication or preface; no notes at the end.

A37a Lectures on certain difficulties felt by Anglicans in submitting to the Catholic Church. London: Burns & Lambert, 1850.

Twelve lectures published separately with the above title, name of publisher, and the number and title of the lecture on each cover.

Lecture I. On the relation of the national church to the nation. pp. 3-28.

Lecture II. The movement of 1833 uncongenial with the national church. pp. 29-55.

Lecture III. Grace in the movement of 1833, not from the national church. pp. 57-80.

Lecture IV. The providential direction of the movement of 1833 not towards the national church. pp. 81-104.

Lecture V. The providential direction of the movement of 1833 not towards a party in the national church. pp. 105-34.

Lecture VI. The providential direction of the movement of 1833 not towards a branch church. pp. 135-63.

Lecture VII. The providential direction of the movement of 1833 not towards a sect. pp. 165-90.

Lecture VIII. Political state of Catholic countries no prejudice to the sanctity of the church. pp. 191-215.

Lecture IX. The religious character of Catholic countries, no prejudice to the sanctity of the church. pp. 217-42.

Lecture X. Differences among Catholics no prejudice to the unity of the church. pp. 243-68.

Lecture XI. Heretical and schismatical bodies no prejudice to the catholicity of the church. pp. 269-94.

Lecture XII. Christian history no prejudice to the apostolicity of the church. pp. 295-325.

A37b Lectures on certain difficulties felt by Anglicans in submitting to the Catholic Church. [On spine: Newman on Anglican difficulties.] London: Burns & Lambert, 1850.

xiv (1), 325 pp.

Individual lectures with separate title pages are bound together with above title page, dedication, preface, and table of contents.

Copy at B.O. with corrections in N's hand.

A37c Lectures on certain difficulties felt by Anglicans in submitting to the Catholic Church. [On spine: Newman on Anglican difficulties, 2nd ed.] Second edition. London: Burns & Lambert, 1850.

xv (1), 325 pp.

A37d Lectures on certain difficulties felt by Anglicans in submitting to the Catholic Church. From the second London edition. New York: Office of New York's Freeman's Journal, 1851.

xii, 396 pp.

American edition.

A37e Lectures on certain difficulties felt by Anglicans in submitting to the Catholic Church. New and revised edition. Dublin: James Duffy, 1857.

xiii (1), 316 pp.

New and revised edition.

Later published as *Difficulties felt by Anglicans in Catholic teaching*, fourth edition, [1872], and *Certain difficulties felt by Anglicans in Catholic teaching* *, [1876], and thereafter as *Certain diff.*, I. See **A15a, A7a,c,e,g.**

A38a Lectures on the history of the Turks in its relation to Christianity by the author of Loss and gain. Dublin: James Duffy; London: Charles Dolman, 1854.

x (1), 295 pp.

Copy at B.O. inscribed by N: "I have read with the greatest interest and pleasure your Lectures on the Turks, in constant admiration of the . . . and *the correctness of your historical views.* Pray let us have another fruit &c. Dollinger to me. July 15, 1854."

Later published as *H.S.*, I. See **A31a,c,k.**

A39a Lectures on justification. London: Printed for J. G. & F. Rivington & J. H. Parker, Oxford, 1838.

xi, 443 pp.

Copy at B.O. inscribed: "John H. Newman March 30. 1838." with corrections in N's hand, some for second edition and others in square brackets since the second edition.

A39b Lectures on justification. Second edition. London: Printed for J. G. F. & J. Rivington & J. H. Parker, Oxford, 1840.
  xi, 453 pp.

A39c Lectures on the doctrine of justification. Third edition. London, Oxford, and Cambridge: Rivingtons, 1874.
  xvi, 404 pp.
  New edition. Advertisement added.
  Copy at B.O. with corrections in N's hand. A list of corrections dated Sept. 30, 1884, on a separate sheet, and pages listed on fly leaf. Also a rough draft "not used" on two opinions put forth in the lectures.

A39d Lectures on the doctrine of justification. Fourth edition. London: Rivingtons, 1885.
  xvi, 404 pp.

A39e Lectures on the doctrine of justification. Fifth edition. London: Rivingtons, 1890. [On spine: Longmans & Co.]
  xvi, 404 pp.

A40a Lectures on the present position of Catholics in England: addressed to the Brothers of the Oratory. London: Burns & Lambert, 1851.
  x (1), 388 pp.
  Burns brought out the lectures, as they were delivered, in the same form and pagination as the first edition, but each with an additional heading, and without the title page and dedication. N also sold printed copies of the lectures in the lecture room. Before the type was broken up, he published these as a cheap edition, called *Lectures on Catholicism in England*. See **A36a**.

A40b Lectures on the present position of Catholics in England: addressed to the Brothers of the Oratory. London: Burns & Lambert, 1851.
  x (1), 388 pp.
  Pp. 197-200—asterisks in place of original passage on Achilli with inscription: "De illis quae sequebantur / posterorum judicium sit. / *In fest. Nativ. S. Joan. Bapt.* / 1852."

A40c Lectures on the present position of Catholics in England: addressed to the Brothers of the Oratory. Second edition. London: Burns & Lambert, 1851.

> x (1), 388 pp.
> Copy at B.O. with contents page, preface, and dedication bound incorrectly; another copy properly bound.

A40d Lectures on the present position of Catholics in England: addressed to the Brothers of the Oratory. Third edition. Dublin: James Duffy, 1857.

> New edition. See Cope.

A40e Lectures on the present position of Catholics in England: addressed to the Brothers of the Oratory. Fourth edition. London: Burns, Oates, & Company, [1872].

> xiii (1), 416 pp.
> New edition. "A correspondence between the Rev. J. H. Newman, D.D. and the bishop of Norwich" added as note.

A40f Lectures on the present position of Catholics in England: addressed to the Brothers of the Oratory in the summer of 1851. Fifth edition. London: Burns, Oates, & Company, [1880].

> xiii (1), 416 pp.

A40g Lectures on the present position of Catholics in England: addressed to the Brothers of the Oratory in the summer of 1851. Sixth edition. London and New York: Longmans, Green, and Co., 1889.

> xiii (1), 416 pp.

A41a Lectures on the prophetical office of the Church, viewed relatively to Romanism and popular Protestantism. London: Printed for J. G. F. Rivington & J. H. Parker, Oxford, 1837.

> xi, 422 pp.
> Copy at B.O. with corrections in N's hand, and inscribed: "John H. Newman March 11, 1837. Keep this copy."

A41b Lectures on the prophetical office of the Church, viewed relatively to Romanism and popular Protestantism. Second edition. London: Printed for J. G. & F. Rivington & J. H. Parker, Oxford, 1838.

xi, 430 pp.

Later published in *V.M.*, I. See **A98a**.

A42a A letter addressed to His Grace the duke of Norfolk on occasion of Mr. Gladstone's recent expostulation. London: B. M. Pickering, 1875.

131 pp.

Two copies at B.O. with corrections in N's hand.

A42b Postscript to A letter addressed to His Grace the duke of Norfolk on occasion of Mr. Gladstone's recent expostulation. London: B. M. Pickering, 1875.

pp. 133-56.

Same as **A72a**.

A42c A letter addressed to His Grace the duke of Norfolk on occasion of Mr. Gladstone's recent expostulation. New edition with postscript on Mr. Gladstone's "Vaticanism." London: B. M. Pickering, 1875.

156 pp.

A42d A letter addressed to His Grace the duke of Norfolk, on occasion of Mr. Gladstone's recent expostulation. New York: The Catholic Publication Society, 1875.

171 pp.

American edition. No postscript.

A42e Postscript to A letter addressed to His Grace the duke of Norfolk, on occasion of Mr. Gladstone's recent expostulation. New York: Catholic Publication Society, 1875.

31 pp. (pp. 173-200).

American edition of Postscript. Same as **A72b**.

A42f A letter addressed to His Grace the duke of Norfolk on occasion of Mr. Gladstone's recent expostulation. Fourth edition with a postscript. London: B. M. Pickering, 1875.

172 pp.

New and corrected edition.

Copy at B.O. with corrections in N's hand, and inscribed: "J.H.N. April 5, 1875."

Later published in *Certain diff.***, [1876], and thereafter in *Certain diff.*, II. See **A7b,d.**

A43a A letter addressed to the Rev. R. W. Jelf, D.D., canon of Christ Church, in explanation of no. 90, in the series called the Tracts for the Times. By the author [signed at the end: J. H. N.]. Oxford: John Henry Parker; London: J. G. F. and J. Rivington, 1841.

30 pp.

A43b A letter addressed to the Rev. R. W. Jelf, D.D., canon of Christ Church, in explanation of no. 90, in the series called the Tracts for the Times. By the author [signed J. H. N. with a postscript]. Second edition. Oxford: John Henry Parker; London: J. G. F. and J. Rivington, 1841.

31 pp.

A43c A letter addressed to the Rev. R. W. Jelf, D.D., canon of Christ Church, in explanation of no. 90, in the series called the Tracts for the Times. By the author [signed J. H. N. with a postscript]. Third edition. Oxford: John Henry Parker; London: J. G. F. and J. Rivington, 1841.

31 pp.

Later published in *V.M.*, II. See **A98a.**

A44a A letter to the Rev. E. B. Pusey, D.D., on his recent Eirenicon. London: Longmans, Green, Reader, and Dyer, 1866.

159 pp.

A44b A letter to the Rev. E. B. Pusey, D.D., on his recent Eirenicon. New York: Lawrence Kehoe, 1866.

86 pp.

American edition.

A44c A letter to the Rev. E. B. Pusey, D.D., on his recent Eirenicon. Second edition. London: Longmans, Green, Reader, and Dyer, 1866.

159 pp.

A44d A letter to the Rev. E. B. Pusey, D.D., on his recent Eirenicon. Third edition. London: Longmans, Green, Reader, and Dyer, 1866.

160 pp.

Later published in *Difficulties felt by Anglicans*, fourth edition, [1872]. Then in *Certain diff.* **, [1876], and thereafter in *Certain diff.*, II. See **A15a, A7b,d.**

A45a [Letter] To my parishioners on occasion of laying the first stone of the church at Littlemore. [Signed: John H. Newman / July 21, 1835.]

4 pp.

Later published in appendix, *Moz.*, II.

A46a A letter to the Rev. Godfrey Faussett, D.D., Margaret Professor of Divinity, on certain points of faith and practice. Oxford: John Henry Parker; London: J. G. and F. Rivington, 1838.

99 pp.

A46b A letter to the Rev. Godfrey Faussett, D.D., Margaret Professor of Divinity, on certain points of faith and practice. Second edition. Oxford: John Henry Parker; London: J. G. F. Rivington, 1838.

104 pp.

Later published in *V.M.*, II. See **A98a.**

A47a A letter to the Right Reverend Father in God, Richard [Bagot], Lord Bishop of Oxford, on occasion of no. 90, in the series called the Tracts for the Times. Oxford: John Henry Parker; London: J. G. F. and J. Rivington, 1841.

47 pp.

Later published in *V.M.*, II. See **A98a.**

A48a Letters and correspondence of John Henry Newman, during his life in the English Church. With a brief autobiography. Edited, at the cardinal's request, by Anne Mozley. 2 vols. London: Longmans, Green, and Co., 1890.

436 pp.; 461 pp.

A49a The life of Apollonius Tyanaeus: with a comparison between the miracles of scripture and those elsewhere related, as regards their respective object, nature, and evidence. Reprinted from the original edition, [n.d.].

pp. 337-97.

Originally published in the *Encyclopaedia metropolitana*, Third Division, 1826. See **C9c**.

Later published in *H.S.*, I. See **A31a,c,k**. Part on miracles put in *Mir.* See **A92a**.

A50a Loss and gain. [Anon.] London: James Burns, 1848.
[iv] , 386 pp.

A50b Loss and gain. [Anon.] Second edition. London: James Burns, 1848.
[iv] , 386 pp.
Advertisement reworded.
Copy at B.O. with corrections in N's hand.

A50c Loss and gain; or the story of a convert . . . by John Henry Newman. Third edition. Dublin: J. Duffy, 1853.
iv, 356 pp.
Listed as given by [C] .

A50d Loss and gain; or the story of a convert. [Anon.] New edition. London: James Burns, 1853.
Listed as given by [C] .

A50e Loss and gain; or the story of a convert. By John Henry Newman. Boston: Patrick Donahue, 1854.
252 pp.
American edition.

A50f Loss and gain; or the story of a convert. By John Henry Newman. Second edition. Boston: Patrick Donahue, 1855.
252 pp.

A50g Loss and gain: or, the story of a convert. [Anon.] Fourth edition. London: Burns and Lambert, 1858.
352 pp.

A50h Loss and gain; or, the story of a convert. [Advertisement signed: J.H.N.] Fifth edition. London: Burns, Lambert, & Oates, 1869.
384 pp.

A50i Loss and gain: the story of a convert. By John Henry Newman. Sixth edition. London: Burns, Oates & Co., Basil Montagu Pickering, 1874.

xi, 432 pp.

New edition. Dedication and another advertisement added.

A50j Loss and gain: the story of a convert. Seventh edition. London: Burns, Oates & Co., 1876.

x, 432 pp.

A50k Loss and gain: the story of a convert. Eighth edition. London: Burns and Oates, 1881.

viii (1), 432 pp.

A50l Loss and gain: the story of a convert. Ninth edition. London: Burns and Oates; New York: Catholic Publication Society Co., 1886.

viii (1), 432 pp.

A51a Make ventures for Christ's sake. A sermon. [Anon.] Oxford: Sold by J. H. Parker; London: by Messrs. Rivington, 1836. [King, Printer, St. Clements.]

15 pp.

A51b Make ventures for Christ's sake. A sermon. [Anon.] First American edition. New York: Doolittle & Vermilye, 1837.

12 pp.

Later published as "The ventures of faith," *P.S.*, IV, and *P.P.S.*, IV. See **A65a-d** and **A69a**.

A52a Memorials of the past. [Dedication signed: J. H. N.] Oxford: W. King, Printer, 1832.

[iv], 108 (1) pp.

"Of the thirty poems the volume contains, Newman himself later reprinted twenty in the *Lyra apostolica* and *Verses on Various Occasions*" (Noel). The following poems were never republished: 3 eclogues: "Spring," "Summer," and "Autumn"; 4 poems to his brothers and sisters on their birthdays: "To M. S. N." [Mary] (My sister on a day so dear), "To C. R. N." [Charles] (A year and more has fled); To H. E. N. [Harriet] (The muse has sway in the truant mind); "To J. C.

N." [Jemima] (I am a tree, whose spring is o'er); "Paraphrase of Ecclesiastes"; "Prologue to the masque of Amyntor" (In times of eld, ere Learning's dawning beam); "Reverie on a journey" (The coachman was seated, the ribbons in hand).

A53a Miscellanies from the Oxford sermons and other writings of John Henry Newman, D.D. London: Strahan & Co., 1870.
[iii], 401 pp.
See *Letters and diaries*, XXVI, 283, 321, 401.

A53b Miscellanies from the Oxford sermons and other writings of John Henry Newman, D.D. Second edition. London: Strahan and Co., 1872.
[iii], 401 pp.

A53c Miscellanies from the Oxford sermons and other writings of John Henry Newman, D.D. London: Daldy, Isbister & Co., 1877.
[iii], 401 pp.

A53d Miscellanies from the Oxford sermons and other writings of John Henry Newman, D.D. New edition. London: W. H. Allen & Co., 1890.
[iii], 401 pp.

A54a The mission of St. Philip Neri. An instruction, delivered in substance in the Birmingham Oratory, January, 1850, and at subsequent times. 1857.
54 pp.
Later published in *O.S.* See **A84a**.

A55a Mr. Kingsley and Dr. Newman: a correspondence on the question whether Dr. Newman teaches that truth is no virtue? [with remarks by J. H. Newman]. London: Longman, Green, Longman, Roberts, and Green, 1864.
34 pp.
Later published in American edition of *Apo.* See **A1c**.

A56a The nature and characteristics of literature: a lecture delivered before the faculty of philosophy and letters, in the

Catholic University, published at the request of the faculty. Dublin: Printed by John F. Fowler, 1858.

40 pp.

Later published as "Literature," *L.U.S.* and *Idea.* See **A35a, A33a.**

A57a The office and work of universities. London: Longman, Brown, Green, and Longmans, 1856.

viii, 384 pp.

Originally published as articles in *The Catholic University Gazette*, I (June 1–Oct. 19, 1854). See **B6a,c,d,f,h-n,q-t,v,x, z,aa,cc.**

A57b The office and work of universities. London: Longman, Green, Longman, and Roberts, 1859.

viii, 384 pp.

Later published as "Rise and progress of universities," *H.S.*, III. See **A31a,b,m.**

A58a On a criticism urged against a Catholic doctrine, by John Henry Cardinal Newman. From "The Contemporary Review" of October, 1885. Birmingham: Martin Billing, Son, and Co., 1889.

33 pp.

Originally published as "The development of religious error, *The Contemporary Review*, XLVIII (Oct. 1885), 457-69. See **B9a.**

Later printed as Head III in *Criticisms urged against certain Catholic doctrines*, in *E.C.P.*, and as Essay III in *S.E.* See **A13a, A28a, A87a.**

A59a On inspiration of scripture, with a postscript, by Cardinal Newman. Birmingham: Martin Billing, Son, and Co. Printers. [Dated at the end: *May*, 1884.]

19 pp.; another copy, 25 pp.

Copies at B.O. with corrections in N's hand seem to be preliminary versions of *What is of obligation for a Catholic to believe concerning the inspiration of the canonical scriptures, being a postscript.* See **A100a.**

A60a Orate pro anima Jacobi Roberti Hope Scott. [Advertisement signed: J.H.N.] [n.p., 1873].

    22 pp.

    Then published as *Sermon preached . . . for the repose of the soul of James Hope Scott*. See **A81a**.

A61a Parochial sermons.

    Note: There were six volumes which went through a number of editions. Subsequent editions are listed after the first edition of each volume. The six volumes were subsequently reprinted as the first six volumes of *Parochial and plain sermons*, 1868. See **A69a**.

A62a Parochial sermons. London: Printed for J. G. & F. Rivington & J. H. Parker, Oxford, 1834.

    xii, 402 pp.

    Copy at B.O. with corrections in N's hand.

A62b Parochial sermons. Vol. I. Second edition. London: Printed for J. F. G. & F. Rivington & J. H. Parker, Oxford, 1835.

    xii, 404 pp.

A62c Parochial sermons. Vol. I. Third edition. London: Printed for J. F. G. & F. Rivington & J. H. Parker, Oxford, 1837.

    xii, 404 pp.

A62d Parochial sermons. Vol. I. Fourth edition. London: Printed for J. F. G. & F. Rivington & J. H. Parker, Oxford, 1840.

    xii, 404 pp.

A62e Parochial sermons. Vol. I. Fifth edition. London: Francis & John Rivington & J. H. Parker, Oxford, 1844.

    xii, 404 pp.

A63a Parochial sermons. Vol. II. For the festivals of the Church. London: Printed for J. G. & F. Rivington & J. H. Parker, Oxford, 1835.

    xix, 451 pp.

A63b Parochial sermons. Vol. II. For the festivals of the Church. Second edition. London: Printed for J. G. & F. Rivington & J. H. Parker, Oxford, 1836.

xv, 455 pp.
Note added.

A63c Parochial sermons. Vol. II. For the festivals of the Church. Third edition. London: Printed for J. G. & F. Rivington & J. H. Parker, Oxford, 1840.
xix, 455 pp.

A63d Parochial sermons. Vol. II. For the festivals of the Church. Fourth edition. London: Printed for J. G. & F. Rivington & J. H. Parker, Oxford, 1843.
xx, 455 pp.

A63e Parochial sermons. Vol. II. For the festivals of the Church. Fifth edition. London: Francis & John Rivington & J. H. Parker, Oxford, 1851.
xx, 455 pp.

A64a Parochial sermons. Vol. III. London: Printed for J. G. & F. Rivington & J. H. Parker, Oxford, 1836.
xv, 424 pp.

A64b Parochial sermons. Vol. III. Second edition. London: Printed for J. G. & F. Rivington & J. H. Parker, Oxford, 1837.
xv, 428 pp.
Advertisement added.

A64c Parochial sermons. Vol. III. Third edition. London: Printed for J. G. & F. Rivington & J. H. Parker, Oxford, 1840.
xv, 440 pp.
Notes added to sermons I and XVI.

A64d Parochial sermons. Vol. III. Fourth edition. London: Francis & John Rivington & J. H. Parker, Oxford, 1844.
xv, 440 pp.

A65a Parochial sermons. Vol. IV. London: Printed for J. G. & F. Rivington & J. H. Parker, Oxford, 1839.
xi, 392 pp.

A65b Parochial sermons. Vol. IV. Second edition. London: Printed for J. G. & F. Rivington & J. H. Parker, Oxford, 1839.
xi, 392 pp.

A65c Parochial sermons. Vol. IV. Third edition. London:.Printed for J. G. & F. Rivington & J. H. Parker, Oxford, 1842.
　xi, 392 pp.

A65d Parochial sermons. Vol. IV. Fourth edition. London: James Burns, 1849.
　xix, 389 pp.
　Advertisement and textual changes added. "The following sermons, written when the author belonged to the Anglican Communion, are so far altered in the present edition, as they contained any thing contrary to Faith and Morals."

A66a Parochial sermons, for the winter quarter, being the weeks between advent Sunday and Lent. Vol. V. London: Printed for J. G. F. & J. Rivington & J. H. Parker, Oxford, 1840.
　xii, 403 pp.

A66b Parochial sermons, for the winter quarter, being the weeks between advent Sunday and Lent. Vol. V. Second edition. London: Printed for J. G. F. & J. Rivington & J. H. Parker, Oxford, 1842.
　xii, 403 pp.

A66c Parochial sermons, for the winter quarter, being the weeks between advent Sunday and Lent. Vol. V. Third edition. London: Printed for Francis & John Rivington & J. H. Parker, Oxford, 1857.
　xii, 403 pp.

A67a Parochial sermons, for the spring quarter, being the weeks between the first Sunday in Lent and Trinity Sunday. Vol. VI. London: Printed for J. G. F. & J. Rivington & J. H. Parker, Oxford, 1842.
　xi, 403 pp.
　Copy at B.O. with textual revision, p. 367.

A67b Parochial sermons, for the spring quarter, being the weeks between the first Sunday in Lent and Trinity Sunday. Vol. VI. Second edition. London: Francis & John Rivington & J. H. Parker, Oxford, 1845.
　xi, 403 pp.

A68a Parochial sermons. Six volumes, London edition, in two vols. New York: D. Appleton and Co.; Philadelphia: George S. Appleton, 1843.

xv, 682 pp.; xiv, 625 pp.

A68b Parochial sermons. Six volumes, London edition, in two vols. New York: D. Appleton and Co., 1848.

xv, 682 pp.; xiv, 625 pp.

A69a Parochial and plain sermons in eight volumes. New edition. [Preface to vol. 1 signed by editor of the volumes: W. J. Copeland.] London, Oxford, and Cambridge: Rivingtons, 1868.

xx, 349 pp.; xv, 402 pp.; xiii, 387 pp.; xii, 343 pp.; xii, 356 pp.; xi, 371 pp.; ix, 257 pp.; viii, 268 pp.

Copies of vols. 1, 2, 5, and 8 at B.O. with corrections in N's hand.

"The first six volumes are reprinted from the six volumes of 'PAROCHIAL SERMONS;' the seventh and eighth formed the fifth volume of 'PLAIN SERMONS, by CONTRIBUTORS TO THE TRACTS FOR THE TIMES,' which was the contribution of its Author to that Series.

"All the Sermons are reprinted from the last Editions of the several volumes, published from time to time by the Messrs. Rivington. . . .

"In conclusion it is right, though scarcely necessary to observe, that the republication of these Sermons by the Editor is not to be considered as equivalent to a re-assertion by their Author of all that they contain; inasmuch as, being printed entire and unaltered, except in the most insignificant particulars, they cannot be free from passages which he certainly now would wish were otherwise, or would, one may be sure, desire to see altered or omitted.

"But the alternative plainly lies between publishing all or nothing, and it appears more to the glory of God and for the cause of religion, to publish all, than to destroy the acceptableness of the Volumes to those for whom they were written by any omissions and alterations" (Preface).

Prefaces, Pusey's note about Lot, and quotation from Hooker, at the end of *P.S.*, III (later editions), and *P.S.*, II, respectively, were not reprinted. Two slight alterations were made in sermon, "Faith and sight," *P.S.*, II. "Intermediate state," *P.S.*, III, would be an example of a sermon, "which, if it were left to me, I certainly should not republish, as it enforces doctrinal views, which I altogether disown and contemn" (*Letters and diaries*, XXIV, 50).

As copies of each volume were sold out, individual volumes were reprinted with new title pages bearing the date of republication. Reimpressions have been checked for the following years:

```
1869 — vols. 1, 4, 5
1870 — vol. 4
1872 — vol. 3
1873 — vols. 2, 5, 8
1875 — vols. 1, 3, 4, 6, 7, 8
1877 — vols. 1, 3, 4
1878 — vols. 6, 7
1879 — vol. 1
1880 — vol. 2
1881 — vols. 3, 6
1882 — vols. 1, 3, 4, 5, 7, 8
1884 — vols. 2, 4
1885 — vol. 3
1887 — vols. 1, 4, 6
1888 — vols. 5, 7, 8
```

A69b Parochial and plain sermons in eight vols. New edition. [Preface to vol. 1 signed: W. J. Copeland.] London, Oxford, and Cambridge: Rivingtons; New York: Scribner, Welford & Co., 1868.

A70a Plain sermons, by contributors to the "Tracts for the Times," 27 series, vol. 5. [Anon.] London: Printed for J. G. F. & J. Rivington, 1843.

iv, 342 pp.

Also listed as **C44a**. See also **C43a**.

Later published as *P.P.S.*, VII and VIII. See **A69a**.

A71a The pope and the revolution: a sermon, preached in the Oratory Church, Birmingham, on Sunday, October 7, 1866. London: Longmans, Green, Reader, and Dyer, 1866.

    48 pp.

    Later published in third and subsequent editions of *O.S.* See **A84c-g**.

A72a Postscript to a letter addressed to His Grace the duke of Norfolk on occasion of Mr. Gladstone's recent expostulation. London: B. M. Pickering, 1875.

    pp. 133-56.

    Also listed as **A42b**. Also published with *A letter to the duke of Norfolk*. See **A42c,f**.

A72b Postscript to a letter to His Grace the duke of Norfolk on occasion of Mr. Gladstone's recent expostulation, and in answer to his "Vaticanism." By John Henry Newman. Together with the decrees and canons of the Vatican Council. New York: The Catholic Publication Society, 1875.

    pp. 173-200 with cover title.

    American edition of *Postscript*. Same as **A42e**.

A73a Relations between medical science and theology. Address delivered to the students in the faculty of medicine of the Catholic University. Published at the request of the faculty. Dublin: Printed by John F. Fowler, 1858.

    40 pp.

    Later published as "Christianity and medical science," in *L.U.S.* and in *Idea*. See **A35a, A33a**.

A74a The restoration of suffragan bishops recommended, as a means of effecting a more equal distribution of episcopal duties, as contemplated by His Majesty's recent ecclesiastical commission. London: Printed for J. G. & F. Rivington & J. H. Parker, Oxford, 1835.

    iv, 52 pp.

    Copy in Opuscula at B.O. with corrections in N's hand. Later published in *V.M.*, II. See **A98a**.

A75a St. Bartholomew's Eve; a tale of the sixteenth century: in two cantos. [Anon.] Oxford: For Munday and Slatter, Herald Office, High Street, 1818.

48 pp.

"Its first canto was published in November 1818; its second in February 1819. The two cantos were subsequently bound together" (Noel).

Copy at B.O. inscribed by N: "This copy was marked at the time of publication (as far as I recollect) with the letters A, B; B standing for B's [Bowden's] part, A for mine, T (I suppose) for both of us together."

A75b St. Bartholomew's Eve; a tale of the sixteenth century. In two cantos. [Anon.] Oxford: Printed and published by Munday and Slatter, 1821.

48 pp.

Copy at B.O. inscribed by N: "Fresh title page, really 1819."

A76a Sanctus Philippus. Birminghamiensis, [n.d., but copy inscribed: "JHN August 17. 1871"].

65 pp.

Contents:

I. The prayer of Baronius.

II. Litaniae de S. Philippo.

III. Decree of Congregation. C.G., Feb. 1, 1861.

IV. Form of admission of a lay brother.

V. Form of admission of a novice.

VI. Form of admission of a Triennial Father.

[VII]. Remarks on the Oratorian vocation.

Seven letters signed: J.H.N.—March 1856. Later published in Placid Murray, *Newman the Oratorian: his unpublished Oratory papers*, pp. 313-46. See **D13**.

A77a The scope and nature of university education. Second edition. London: Longman, Green, Longman, and Roberts, 1859.

xxvii (1), 351 pp.

Originally published as *Discourses on university education* (pamphlets), and *Discourses on the scope and nature of university education*, 1852. See **A17a,b**.

New and revised edition. Discourse 5 was dropped, and Discourses 1 and 2 were rewritten as Discourse 1. Appendix was also dropped.

Later published in *Idea*. See A33a.

A78a The second spring. A sermon preached in the synod of Oscott, on Tuesday, July 13th, 1852. London, Dublin, and Derby: Thomas Richardson and Son, 1852.

30 pp.

Later published in *O.S.* See **A84a**.

A79a Selection adapted to the seasons of the ecclesiastical year from the parochial and plain sermons of John Henry Newman, B.D., sometime vicar of St. Mary's Oxford. Preface by W. J. C[opeland]. London, Oxford, and Cambridge: Rivingtons, 1878.

xix, 468 pp.

Copy at B.O. inscribed: "J. H. Newman / Decr 3. 1878," and corrections in N's hand.

The sermons included are: *P.P.S.*, I, 1, 2, 5, 9, 17, 22, 25, 26; II, 28; III, 9, 10, 11; IV, 2, 3, 6, 13, 14, 15, 17, 19, 20, 22, 23; V, 5, 6, 9, 16, 19, 20, 22, 23, 24; VI, 2, 4, 7, 15, 16, 17, 19, 22; VII, 1, 2, 3, 4, 10, 14, 15; VIII, 2, 5, 6, 9, 11, 16, 17.

A79b Selection adapted to the seasons of the ecclesiastical year from the parochial and plain sermons of John Henry Newman, B.D., sometime vicar of St. Mary's Oxford. Preface by W. J. C[opeland]. Second edition. London: Rivingtons, 1882.

xix, 468 pp.

A79c Selection adapted to the seasons of the ecclesiastical year from the parochial and plain sermons of John Henry Newman, B.D., sometime vicar of St. Mary's Oxford. Preface by W. J. C[opeland]. Third edition. London: Rivingtons, 1886.

xix, 468 pp.

A79d Selection adapted to the seasons of the ecclesiastical year from the parochial and plain sermons of John Henry Newman, B.D., sometime vicar of St. Mary's Oxford. Preface by W. J. C[opeland]. Fourth edition. London: Rivingtons, 1889.

xix, 468 pp.

A79e Selection adapted to the seasons of the ecclesiastical year from the parochial and plain sermons of John Henry Newman, B.D., sometime vicar of St. Mary's Oxford. Preface by W. J. C[opeland]. Fifth edition. London and New York: Longmans, Green, and Co., 1891.

    xix, 468 pp.

A80a Selection from the first four volumes of parochial sermons. London: Printed for J. G. F. & J. Rivington & J. H. Parker, Oxford, 1841.

    xi, 462 pp.

    Contents:
        I. God's commandments not grievous (I,8).
        II. The religious use of excited feelings (I,9).
        III. Religious emotion (I,14).
        IV. Promising without doing (I,13).
        V. Christian repentance (III,7).
        VI. Contracted views in religion (III,8).
        VII. Obedience the remedy for religious perplexity (I, 18).
        VIII. Faith and obedience (III,6).
        IX. Knowledge of God's will without obedience (I,3).
        X. Profession without practice (I,10).
        XI. Profession without hypocrisy (I,11).
        XII. Profession without ostentation (I,12).
        XIII. Times of private prayer (I,19).
        XIV. Forms of private prayer (I,20).
        XV. Reliance on religious observances (IV,5).
        XVI. Sins of ignorance and weakness (I,7).
        XVII. Moral consequences of single sins (IV,3).
        XVIII. Submission to church authority (III,14).
        XIX. The gainsaying of Korah (IV,18).
        XX. Obedience without love, as instanced in the character of Balaam (IV,2).
        XXI. Christian reverence (I,23).
        XXII. A particular providence as revealed in the gospel (III,9).
        XXIII. The danger of riches (II,28).
        XXIV. Christian manhood (I,26).

> XXV. Watching (IV,22).
> XXVI. The greatness and littleness of human life (IV, 14).
> XXVII. The invisible world (IV,13).

A81a Sermon preached in the London Church of the Jesuit Fathers at the requiem mass for the repose of the soul of James Robert Hope Scott. . . . London: Burns, Oates, and Co., 1873.
22 pp.
First printed as *Orate*. See **A60a**.
Later published in fourth and subsequent editions of *O.S.*, "In the world, but not of the world." See **A84d-h**.

A82a Sermons, bearing on subjects of the day. London: Printed for J. G. F. & J. Rivington & J. H. Parker, Oxford, 1843.
xv, 464 pp.
Copy at B.O. inscribed: "John H Newman / Dec 8. 1843," with corrections in N's hand. The advertisement in this edition begins: "The Sermons which follow were all preached in St. Mary's, Oxford." N notes: "This mistake stopped the publication. Gladstone found it out for me." Changed in second edition to "the author's late Parish."

A82b Sermons, bearing on subjects of the day. Second edition. London: Printed for J. G. F. & J. Rivington & J. H. Parker, Oxford, 1844.
xv, 464 pp.

A82c Sermons bearing on subjects of the day. New York: D. Appleton; Philadelphia: George S. Appleton, 1844.
xii, 357 pp.
American edition.

A82d Sermons bearing on subjects of the day. New edition. [Preface by W. J. Copeland.] London, Oxford, Cambridge: Rivingtons, 1869.
xxi, 424 pp.
New edition. Added in this edition is a list of dates when *P.P.S.* and *Sermons on subjects of the day* were first preached or written.

A82e Sermons bearing on subjects of the day. New edition. [Preface by W. J. Copeland.] London, Oxford, Cambridge: Rivingtons, 1871.

> xxi, 424 pp.

A82f Sermons bearing on subjects of the day. New edition. [Preface by W. J. Copeland.] London, Oxford, Cambridge: Rivingtons, 1873.

> xxi, 424 pp.

A82g Sermons bearing on subjects of the day. [Preface by W. J. Copeland.] New edition. London, Oxford, and Cambridge: Rivingtons, 1879.

> xxi, 424 pp.

A82h Sermons bearing on subjects of the day. New edition. [Preface by W. J. Copeland.] London: Rivingtons, 1885.

> xxi, 424 pp.

A83a Sermons, chiefly on the theory of religious belief, preached before the University of Oxford. London: Printed for J. G. F. & J. Rivington & J. H. Parker, Oxford, 1843.

> viii, 354 pp.

A83b Sermons, chiefly on the theory of religious belief preached before the University of Oxford. Second edition. London: Francis and John Rivington; Oxford: J. H. Parker, 1844.

> viii, 354 pp.
>
> Text at B.O. with corrections in N's hand.
>
> Later published as *Fifteen sermons preached before the University of Oxford*. See **A29a**.

A84a Sermons preached on various occasions. London: Burns and Lambert; Paris and Tournai: Casterman, 1857. The right of translation is reserved.

> x, 284 pp.

A84b Sermons preached on various occasions. Second edition. London: Burns and Lambert, 1858. The right of translation is reserved.

> x, 331 pp.

A84c Sermons preached on various occasions. Third edition. London: Burns, Oates, & Co., 1870. The right of translation is reserved.

xv, 319 pp.

New edition. P.S. added: "He has added to the Third Edition two Sermons, published since the Second, and both written before delivery ['The tree beside the waters'; 'The pope and the revolution']." See **A91a, A71a.** Notes added on sermons 9, 13, 14.

A84d Sermons preached on various occasions. Fourth edition. London: Burns, Oates, & Co., 1874.

xi, 337 pp.

Sermon on Hope Scott, "In the world, but not of the world," added in this edition. See **A60a, A81a.**

A84e Sermons preached on various occasions. Fifth edition. London: Burns & Oates, 1881. The right of translation is reserved.

xi, 337 pp.

A84f Sermons preached on various occasions. Sixth edition. London: Burns and Oates, Limited; New York: Catholic Publication Society Co., 1887.

xi, 337 pp.

A84g Sermons preached on various occasions. Sixth edition. London and New York: Longmans, Green, and Co., 1891.

xi, 337 pp.

A84h Sermons preached on various occasions. New edition. London and New York: Longmans, Green, and Co., 1892.

xi, 337 pp.

Advertisement reads: "This edition contains the few verbal corrections made by the author for insertion in the next Reprint."

A85a Six selections from the writings of John Henry Newman, D.D., by a late member of Oriel College, Oxford. Dorchester: Printed by James Foster, 4, Cornhill; London: Hamilton, Adams, & Co., 32 Paternoster Row, 1874.

8 pp.

A86a Speech of His Eminence Cardinal Newman on the reception of the "Biglietto" at Cardinal Howard's palace in Rome on the 12th of May, 1879. With the address of the English-speaking Catholics in Rome and His Eminence's reply to it, at the English College on the 14th of May, 1879. Rome: Libreria Spithöver, 1879.

> 10 (2) pp.
>> "Biglietto" speech is reprinted in Ward, II, 459-62.

A87a Stray essays on controversial subjects, variously illustrated. [Private [*sic*], 1890.

> iv, 107 pp.
>> Contents:
>>> Essay I. Inspiration in its relation to revelation.
>>>> Originally published as "On the inspiration of scripture," *The Nineteenth Century*, XV (Feb. 1884), 185-99. See **B14a**.
>>> Essay II. Further illustrations.
>>>> Originally published as *What is of obligation for a Catholic to believe.* See **A100a, A59a**.
>>> Essay III. Revelation in its relation to faith.
>>>> Originally published as "The development of religious error," *Contemporary Review*, XLVIII (Oct. 1885), 457-69, and postscript printed with *The development of religious error.* See **B9a, A14a, A58a, A13a, A28a**.
>> Essays I and II are reprinted in John Henry Newman, *On the inspiration of scripture*, edited with an introduction by J. Derek Holmes and Robert Murray, S.J. (London, etc.: Geoffrey Chapman, 1967). Essay III is reprinted in *The theological papers.* See **D18**.

A88a Suggestions respectfully offered to certain resident clergymen of the university, in behalf of the Church Missionary Society, by a Master of Arts [i.e., J.H.N.]. Oxford: Printed by H. Cooke, 1830.

> 16 pp.
>> Copy in Opuscula at B.O. with corrections in N's hand.
>> Later published in *V.M.*, II. See **A98a**.

A89a The Tamworth reading room: Letters on an address delivered by Sir Robert Peel, Bart, M.P. on the establishment of a reading room at Tamworth. By Catholicus [i.e., J.H.N.]. Originally published in the *Times*, and since revised and corrected by the author. London: John Mortimer, 1841.

42 pp.

Originally published in *The Times*, 5, 9, 10, 12, 20, 22, 26, Feb. 1841. See **B19a**.

Copy in Opuscula at B.O. with corrections in N's hand. Later published in *D.A.* See **A18a**.

A90a Tracts theological and ecclesiastical. London: Basil Montagu Pickering, 1874.

viii, 405 pp.

Contents:

I. Dissertatiunculae quatuor critico-theologicae.

Originally published as *Dissertatiunculae quaedam critico-theologicae.* See **A19a**.

II. Causes of the rise and successes of Arianism (February 1872).

III. The heresy of Apollinaris (from notes, dated August 22, 1835).

IV. On St. Cyril's formula, μία φύσις σεσαρκωμένη.

Originally published as "On the formula μία φύσις σεσαρκωμένη," *The Atlantis*, I, no. 2 (July 1858), 330-61. See **B1b**.

V. The history of the text of the Rheims and Douay version of holy scripture.

Originally published as "The text of the Rheims and Douay version of holy scripture," *The Rambler*, I, n.s. (July 1859), 145-69. See **B16g**.

A90b Tracts theological and ecclesiastical. Second edition. London: Pickering and Co., 1881.

vi (1), 445 pp.

Copy at B.O. inscribed: "to T. A. Pope" with inserted paper in N's hand: "1883 correction vid. p. 299."

Another copy at B.O. with note: "This is the copy with the Cardinal's last corrections. WN July 10/91."

Contents:

I. Dissertatiunculae quatuor critico-theologicae.

II. On the text of the Epistles of St. Ignatius.

III. Causes of the rise and successes of Arianism.

IV. The heresy of Apollinaris.

V. St. Cyril's formula, μία φύσις σεσαρκωμένη.

VI. The ordo de tempore in the breviary.

VII. History of the text of the Douay version of scripture.

The title page before each section gives the title as listed in **A90a.**

Two tracts are added to this edition:

1. On the text of the seven Epistles of St. Ignatius which appeared as a note to the "Theology of St. Ignatius," Essay V in *Ess.*, I (1st–4th eds.). It was dropped from the fifth edition of *Ess.* I. See **A27a.**

2. The ordo de tempore in the breviary.
   Originally published as "The ordo de tempore in the Roman breviary" in *The Atlantis*, V (Feb. 1870), 1-12. See **B1d.**

A90c Tracts theological and ecclesiastical. Second edition. London: Burns & Oates, Limited; New York: Catholic Publication Society Co., [1883(?)].

vi (1), 445 pp.

Postscript on p. 299: "May 2, 1883.—My attention having been accidentally called to certain passages in this Tract iii., I have been led to ask myself whether I have always succeeded in bringing out my real meaning with that distinctness which was imperative on so important a subject, and the more so because of the reverence due to the times and persons of whom I had to treat.

"Then I reflected that a fresh edition of the Volume, in which I might avail myself of the opportunity of revision, could hardly be expected in my lifetime.

"The result has been that I have made at once such alterations in the foregoing pages as I felt to be necessary, without waiting for a future which might never come to me. / J.H.N."

A90d Tracts theological and ecclesiastical. Third edition. London and New York: Longmans, Green, and Co., 1891.
> vi (1), 445 pp.

A91a The tree beside the waters. A sermon preached in the chapel of St. Mary's College, Oscott, on Friday, November 11, 1859, at the funeral of the Right Rev. Henry Weedall, D.D. . . . published at the request of the bishops, clergy, and gentry present. London: Burns and Lambert, [n.d.].
> 24 pp.
> Later published in third and subsequent editions of *O.S.* See **A84c**.

A92a Two essays on scripture miracles and on ecclesiastical. Second edition. London: Basil Montagu Pickering, 1870.
> xi, 393 pp.
> Copy at B.O. with corrections on p. 347 in N's hand.
> Contents:
>> Essay I. The miracles of scripture.
>>> Originally published in "The life of Apollonius of Tyanaeus with a comparison between the miracles of scripture and those elsewhere related, as regards their respective object, nature, and evidence," *Encyclopaedia metropolitana*, Third Division, pp. 337-97, but only pp. 356-97. See **C9c**.
>> Essay II. Miracles of early ecclesiastical history.
>>> Originally published as "Essay on the miracles recorded in ecclesiastical history," the preface to *The ecclesiastical history of M. L'Abbé Fleury*, 1842, and printed separately in 1843. See **C17a, A26a**.

A92b Two essays on biblical and on ecclesiastical miracles. Third edition. London: Basil Montagu Pickering, 1873.
> viii, 400 pp.
> Index added.

A92c Two essays on biblical and on ecclesiastical miracles. Fourth edition. London: Basil Montagu Pickering, 1875.
> xi, 400 pp.

A92d Two essays on biblical and on ecclesiastical miracles. Fifth edition. London: Pickering and Co., 1881.

   xi, 400 pp.
   New impression.

A92e Two essays on biblical and on ecclesiastical miracles. Fifth edition. London: Longmans, Green & Co., 1885.

   xi, 400 pp.

A92f Two essays on biblical and on ecclesiastical miracles. Sixth edition. London: Longmans, Green, and Co., 1886.

   xi, 400 pp.
   New impression.

A92g Two essays on biblical and on ecclesiastical miracles. Seventh edition. London and New York: Longmans, Green, and Co., 1888.

   xi, 400 pp.
   New impression.

A92h Two essays on biblical and on ecclesiastical miracles. Eighth edition. London and New York: Longmans, Green, and Co., 1890.

   xi, 400 pp.
   New impression.

A92i Two essays on biblical and on ecclesiastical miracles. Ninth edition. London and New York: Longmans, Green, and Co., 1890.

   xi, 400 pp.
   New impression.

A93a Two letters addressed to the "Christian Observer," published in that magazine in 1821 & 1822. [Anon.] Privately reprinted, 1871.

   See **B7a,b.**

A94a Two sermons preached in the Church of S. Aloysius, Oxford, by J. H. Cardinal Newman, on Trinity Sunday, 1880. Printed for private circulation [by James Parker and Co., Oxford].

   28 pp.

A95a Verses for penitents. Privately printed, 1860.

Frederick Chapman, *The Poems of John Henry Newman afterwards cardinal* (London and New York: John Lane, [n.d.]), p. xvi, mentions this work but adds: "It has proved impossible to obtain a sight of this opusculum, but according to Mr. W. S. Lilly, it contained nothing which did not re-appear in 'Verses on various occasions.' "

A96a Verses on religious subjects. [Anon.] Dublin: James Duffy, 1853.

viii, 141 pp.

"It contains thirty-eight original poems by Newman, together with translations by him of thirty-five Latin hymns (thirty-four from the Roman Breviary and one from the Parisian), and a translation of the section of St. Bede's *Metrical History of St. Cuthbert* which deals with Ethelwald. Of the thirty-eight original poems, three ('The Trance of Time,' 'A Thanksgiving,' and 'A Voice from Afar') had already appeared in *Memorials,* the *British Magazine*, and *Lyra Apostolica.* One, 'Temptation,' had appeared in the *British Magazine* only, and twenty-three were in both the *British Magazine* and *Lyra.* Thus, only eleven of the poems were printed for the first time, all of them had been written since 1849. These new poems were for the most part hymns to the Blessed Virgin and St. Philip Neri. The earlier poems were carefully selected to give no offense to the Catholics to whom the little volume was directed in the Advertisement" (Noel, pp. xxiii-xxiv).

The following poems were published for the first time in *VRS*:

1. Candlemas (A song) (The angel-lights of Christmas morn)
2. The pilgrim queen (A song) (There sat a lady)
3. The month of Mary (A song) (Green are the leaves, and sweet the flowers)
4. The queen of seasons (A song for an inclement May) (All is divine)
5. St. Philip Neri in his mission (A song) (In the far north our lot is cast)

6. St. Philip in himself (A song) (The holy monks, conceal'd from men)

7. St. Philip in his God (Philip, on thee the glowing ray)

8. The holy Trinity (The one true faith, the ancient creed)

9. Guardian angel (My oldest friend, mine from the hour)

10. The golden prison (Weep not for me, when I am gone)

11. St. Philip in his school (This is the saint of sweetness and compassion)

All of the above with the exception of "The holy Trinity" were subsequently published in *V.V.* See **A97a**.

A97a Verses on various occasions. [Dedication signed: J.H.N.] London: Burns, Oates, & Co., 1868.

xi, 340 pp.

"Eighteen of these had been published in *Memorials of the Past*; eighty-eight were from the *Lyra Apostolica*; five were translations from St. Gregory Nazianzen which Newman had first made for his *Church of the Fathers*; thirty-five were translations of Latin hymns first published in *Verses on Religious Subjects*; one was the translation of St. Bede's 'Ethelwald'; sixteen were poems written since his conversion. The one hundred and sixty-fourth poem was the *Dream*. Of the sixteen poems written since 1845, only three were published for the first time, 'St. Philip in His Disciples,' 'For the Dead,' and 'The Two Worlds.' Ten had already been printed in *Verses on Religious Subjects*; two came from his novel *Callista* (1856); and one, 'Valentine for [*sic*] a Little Girl' had appeared in the *Month* for June 1865" (Noel, p. xxvii).

Before the volume had gone into a second edition, "an appendix, to be included in the unsold copies of the first edition, was published. For it Newman wrote a covering statement in which he explained, 'The favour with which his Volume has been received, and the wish of friends, have led the Author to venture on the publication of the following additional compositions, which, for one reason or another, it did not enter into his mind, in the first instance, to publish.' The appendix contained six poems, 'Solitude' (a somewhat revised excerpt from *St. Bartholomew's Eve*), 'My Lady Nature and Her Daughters' from *Memorials of the Past*, and 'Bondage,' 'The Watchman,' 'Absolution,' and 'Separation of Friends' from the *Lyra Apostolica*" (Noel, p. xxviii).

". . . in printing the *Appendix* of Verses to my second Edition, . . . they [Rivingtons] left out the last 4 out of the 20 pages, and *so* it was published before I knew of it" (*Letters and diaries*, XXIV, 96).

A97b Verses on various occasions. [Dedication signed: J.H.N.] Boston: Patrick Donahoe, 1868.

   xii, 340 pp.

A97c Verses on various occasions. [Dedication signed: J.H.N.] London: Burns, Oates, & Co., 1868.

   xii, 368 pp.

   Includes poems of first edition, an appendix, an index of first lines, and two poems not published before, "To Edward Caswall" and "St. Michael" (Noel).

A97d Verses on various occasions. [Dedication signed: J.H.N.] Third edition. London: Burns, Oates, & Co., 1869.

   xv, 368 pp.

A97e Verses on various occasions. London: Burns, Oates, & Co., 1874.

   xiv, 376 pp.

   Added "Superstition," "Sympathy," "Reverence," and "Samaria."

   Copy at B.O. with corrections in N's hand.

A97f Verses on various occasions. London: Burns, Oates, & Co., 1880.

   xiv, 376 pp.

   Copy at B.O. with corrections in N's hand on pp. 85, 332, 362, 363.

A97g Verses on various occasions. London: Burns, Oates, & Co., 1883.

   xiv, 376 pp.

A97h Verses on various occasions. London and New York: Longmans, Green, and Co., 1888.

> xv, 389 pp.
>
> Added "My birthday" from *Memorials of the past* and two Appendixes:
>> Appendix I.
>>> 1. Ad Vesperas.
>>> 2. Ad Laudes.
>> Appendix II.
>>> 1. Prologus in Phormionem.
>>>   Translation of the above.
>>> 2. Prologus in Pincernam.
>>> 3. Prologus in Andriam.

A97i Verses on various occasions. New edition. London and New York: Longmans, Green, and Co., 1889.

> xv, 389 pp.

A97j Verses on various occasions. New edition. London and New York: Longmans, Green, and Co., 1890.

> xv, 389 pp.

A98a The via media of the Anglican Church. Illustrated in lectures, letters, and tracts written between 1830 and 1841. In two volumes, with a preface and notes. London: Basil Montagu Pickering, 1877.

> xciv (1), 355 pp.; (i), 419 pp.
>
> Copy at B.O. inscribed: "John H. Newman/Aug. 15, 1877" with corrections in N's hand.
>
> Contents:
>> Vol. I. Lectures on the prophetical office of the Church viewed relatively to Romanism and popular Protestantism.
>>
>> New edition with preface added ("Preface to the third edition"). See **A41a,b** for previous publication.
>> Vol. II. Occasional letters and tracts.
>>
>> *Note:* The title page before each work gives a fuller title. Those of items I and II are significant. Numbering of contents is as in subsequent editions.

I. Suggestions in behalf of the Church Missionary Society, 1830. [Half-title page:] Suggestions respectfully offered to individual resident clergymen of the university, in behalf of the Church Missionary Society, by a Master of Arts. 1830. (*Not published, but sent to a certain number of residents.*)

Originally printed as *Suggestions respectfully offered to certain resident clergymen.* See **A88a**.

II. Via media 1834. [Half-title page:] Via Media (*Being nos.* 38 *and* 40 *of* Tracts for the Times.) 1834.

Originally published as Tracts 38 and 41 (not 40). See **C69a, C70a**.

III. Restoration of suffragan bishops, 1835.

Originally published separately. See **A74a**.

IV. On the mode of conducting the controversy with Rome, 1836 (being no. 71 of Tracts for the Times).

Originally published as *On the controversy with the Romanists*, Tract 71. See **C73a**.

V. Letter to a magazine in behalf of Dr. Pusey's Tracts on holy baptism, 1837.

Originally published as "Letter from the Rev. J. H. Newman upon the Oxford tracts, with remarks upon it," *The Christian Observer*, XXXVII (Feb. and March 1837), 114-26; 141-45. See **B7c**. Then as Tract 82. See **C79a**.

VI. Letter to the Margaret Professor of Divinity on Mr. R. H. Froude's statements on the Holy Eucharist, 1838.

Originally published as *Letter to the Rev. Godfrey Faussett, D.D., Margaret Professor of Divinity.* See **A46a**.

VII. Remarks on certain passages in the Thirty-nine Articles, 1841.

Originally published with same title as Tract 90. See **C83a**.

VIII. Letter to Dr. Jelf in explanation of the foregoing remarks, with documentary matter consequent thereupon, 1841.

Originally published as *A letter addressed to the Rev. R. W. Jelf, D.D.* See **A43a.**

IX. Letter to the bishop of Oxford on the same subject, 1841.

Originally published as *A letter to the Right Reverend Father in God, Richard, Lord Bishop of Oxford.* See **A47a.**

X. Retractation of anti-Catholic statements, 1843–1845.

Originally published as "Oxford and Rome," *The Conservative Journal*, 28 Jan. 1843. See **B8a.** Then in "Appendix," *The Dublin Review*, XIV (Feb. 1843), 271-75. See **B10a.** Then in advertisement to *Dev.* (1st and 2d eds.). See **A25a,b,c.**

A98b The via media of the Anglican church. Illustrated in lectures, letters, and tracts written between 1830 and 1841. In two volumes, with a preface and notes. Vol. I. London: Pickering and Co., 1882.

xciv (1), 355 pp.

New edition.

A98c The via media of the Anglican church. Illustrated in lectures, letters, and tracts written between 1830 and 1841. In two volumes, with a preface and notes. Vol. II. London: Pickering and Co., 1884.

[ii], 433 pp.

Note added at end.

Copy at B.O. with corrections in N's hand (not incorporated in 1885 edition).

A98d The via media of the Anglican church. Illustrated in lectures, letters, and tracts written between 1830 and 1841. In two volumes, with a preface and notes. London: Longmans, Green, and Co., 1885.

xciv (1), 355 pp.; [ii], 433 pp.

A98e The via media of the Anglican church. Illustrated in lectures, letters, and tracts written between 1830 and 1841. In two volumes, with a preface and notes. London and New York: Longmans, Green, and Co., 1888.

xciv (1), 355 pp.; [ii], 433 pp.

New impression.

A98f The via media of the Anglican church. Illustrated in lectures, letters, and tracts written between 1830 and 1841. In two volumes, with a preface and notes. London and New York: Longmans, Green, and Co., 1891.

xciv (1), 355 pp.; [ii], 433 pp.

A99a [Vice-Chancellor.] "Mr. Vice-Chancellor, I write this respectfully to inform you. . . ." A broadside acknowledging the authorship of Tract 90, signed John H. Newman, Oriel College, March 16, 1841.

Later reprinted in *V.M.*, II. See **A98a**.

A100a What is of obligation for a Catholic to believe concerning the inspiration of the canonical scriptures, being a postscript to an article in the February no. of the "Nineteenth Century Review," in answer to Professor Healy. London: Burns and Oates, [May, 1884 at end].

25 pp.

See **A59a** for preliminary versions of this work.

The original article was "On the inspiration of scripture," *The Nineteenth Century*, XV (Feb. 1884), 185-99. See **B14a**. Healy's criticism appeared in the *Irish Ecclesiastical Record,* 3d ser., V (March 1884), entitled "Cardinal Newman on the inspiration of scripture."

Later printed as Head II in *Criticisms urged against certain Catholic doctrines*, in *E.C.P.*, and as Essay II in *S.E.* See **A13a, A28a, A87a**.

B

Publications in Periodicals and Newspapers

Note: Under each periodical or newspaper, articles are generally listed in chronological order except where the article is continued in several issues and in the case of the *British Magazine*, where they are listed alphabetically. Notices of books, correspondence, etc., are listed after articles. The titles of periodicals and newspapers are entered with numbering **B1, B2, B3**, etc. The articles in a given periodical are noted by the addition of small letters, e.g., **B1a, B1b, B1c,** etc.

B1 *The Atlantis: A Register of Literature and Science.*
Conducted by Members of the Catholic University of Ireland

B1a "The mission of the Benedictine order," signed: Very Rev. John H. Newman, D.D., I, no. 1 (Jan. 1858), 1-49 (to be continued).
  Later published as "The mission of St. Benedict," *H.S.*, II. See **A31a,d,1**.

B1b "On the formula, μία φύσις σεσαρκωμένη," signed: Very Rev. John H. Newman, D.D., I, no. 2 (July 1858), 330-61.
  Later published as "St. Cyril's formula, μία φύσις σεσαρκωμένη," *T.T.* See **A90a**.

B1c "The Benedictine centuries," signed: Very Rev. John H. Newman, D.D., II, no. 3 (Jan. 1859), 1-43.
  Later published as "The Benedictine schools," *H.S.*, II. See **A31a,d,1**.

B1d "The ordo de tempore in the Roman breviary," signed: Very Rev. John H. Newman, D.D., V, no. 9 (Feb. 1870), 1-12.
  Later published as "The ordo de tempore in the Roman breviary," *T.T.* (2d ed. and thereafter). See **A90b**.

B2 *The British Critic. Quarterly Theological Review and Ecclesiastical Record*

B2a "Le Bas' *Life of Archbishop Laud*," XVIII (April 1836), 354-80.

B2b *"The Brothers' controversy — apostolical tradition*," XIX (July 1836), 166-99.
Later published as "Apostolical tradition," *Ess.*, I (beginning with the 5th ed., 1885, and thereafter). See **A27e.**

B2c "Burton's *History of the Christian Church*," XIX (July 1836), 209-31.

B2d "Dr. Wiseman's *Lectures on the Catholic Church*," XIX (Oct. 1836), 373-403.

B2e *"The life of Augustus Herman Franké*," XXI (July 1837), 94-116.
Copy at B.O. has note: "The last 2½ pages are Pusey's in substance. J.H.N."

B2f *"Affairs of Rome*," XXI (Oct. 1837), 261-83.
Later published as "The fall of de la Mennais," *Ess.*, I. See **A27a.**

B2g *"Geraldine—A tale of conscience*," XXIV (July 1838), 61-82.

B2h *"Memorials of Oxford*," XXIV (July 1838), 133-46.
Later published as "Medieval Oxford," *H.S.*, III. See **A31a,b,m.**

B2i *"Exeter Hall*," XXIV (July 1838), 190-211.

B2j "Palmer's *Treatise on the Church of Christ*," XXIV (Oct. 1838), 347-72.
Later published as "Palmer's view of faith and unity," *Ess.*, I. See **A27a.**

B2k "Jacobson's *Apostolical Fathers — Ignatius*," XXV (Jan. 1839), 49-76.
Later published as "The theology of St. Ignatius," *Ess.*, I. See **A27a.**

B2l "Elliott's *Travels*," XXV (April 1939), 305-20.

B2m *"State of religious parties,"* XXV (April 1839), 396-426.
Later published as "Prospects of the Anglican Church," *Ess.*, I. See **A27a**.

B2n *"The American Church,"* XXVI (Oct. 1839), 281-343.
Later published as "The Anglo-American Church," *Ess.*, I. See **A27a**.

B2o *"Mr. Taylor versus Nicolas Ferrar,"* XXVI (Oct. 1839), 440-57.
In Opuscula at B.O., N has note: "only partly JHN." N's list at the B.O. gives "possibly R.F. Wilson, co-author."

B2p "Brewer—*Court of King James the First,"* XXVII (Jan. 1840), 24-39.
Autograph list at Pusey House gives both Newman and Brewer, each with a "?" In Opuscula at B.O., N includes only p. 39.

B2q *"Catholicity of the English Church,"* XXVII (Jan. 1840), 40-88.
Later published as "The catholicity of the Anglican Church," *Ess.*, II. See **A27a**.

B2r *"Persecution of Protestants in Germany,"* XXVIII (July 1840), 160-76.

B2s *"Memoir of the countess of Huntingdon,"* XXVIII (Oct. 1840), 263-95.
Later published as "Selina, countess of Huntingdon," *Ess.*, I. See **A27a**.

B2t "Todd's *Discourses on the prophecies relating to Antichrist,"* XXVIII (Oct. 1840), 391-440.
Later published as "The Protestant idea of Antichrist," *Ess.*, II. See **A27a**.

B2u "Milman's *History of Christianity,"* XXIX (Jan. 1841), 71-114.
Later published as "Milman's view of Christianity," *Ess.*, II. See **A27a**.

B2v "Bowden's *Life of Gregory VII—Reformation of the eleventh century*," XXIX (April 1841), 280-331.

Later published as "The reformation of the eleventh century," *Ess.*, II. See **A27a**.

B2w *"Private judgment,"* XXX (July 1841), 100-134.

Later published as "Private judgment," *Ess.*, II. See **A27a**.

B2x *"Catena aurea of St. Thomas,"* XXX (July 1841), 197-214.

In Opuscula at B.O., N breaks off at p. 200.

B2y *"Works of the late Rev. J. Davison,"* XXXI (April 1842), 367-401.

Later published as "John Davison, Fellow of Oriel," *Ess.*, II. See **A27a**.

B2z "Notices of Books" as given in Opuscula at B.O.

XXIV (July 1838), 230-38.
XXIV (Oct. 1838), 484-92.
XXV (Jan. 1839), 249-56.
XXV (April 1839), 499-504.
XXVI (July 1839), 245-54.
XXVI (Oct. 1839), 508-14.
XXVII (Jan. 1840), 243-48.
XXVII (April 1840), 473-80.
XXVIII (July 1840), 258-62.
XXVIII (Oct. 1840), 523-30.
XXIX (Jan. 1841), 240-48.
XXIX (April 1841), 491-96.
XXX (July 1841), 244-52.

B3 *British Magazine and Monthly Register of Religious and Ecclesiastical Information, Parochial History, and Documents Respecting the State of the Poor, Progress of Education, etc.*

B3a "Centralization," VI (Nov. 1834), 514-17.

B3b "The convocation of the province of Canterbury."

No. I. VI (Nov. 1834), 517-24.
No. II. VI (Dec. 1834), 637-47.
No. III. VII (Jan. 1835), 33-41.
No. IV. VII (Feb. 1835), 145-54.

No. V. VII (March 1835), 259-68.
Later published as "Convocation of Canterbury," *H.S.*, III.
See **A31a,b,m.**

B3c "Home thoughts abroad."
No. I. V (Jan. 1834), 1-11, (Feb. 1834), 121-31.
No. II. IX (March 1836), 237-48; (April 1836), 357-69.
The first part includes a poem, "Far sadder musing on the traveller falls," later published in *Lyra apostolica* under the title "Rome." See **C33a.** Also, "Now, journeying westward, evermore."

No. II was later published as "How to accomplish it," *D.A.*
See **A18a.**

B3d "Letters on the Church of the Fathers."
No. I. [signed N]. IV (Oct. 1833), 421-28.
No. II. [signed N]. IV (Nov. 1833), 540-45.
No. III [signed N]. IV (Dec. 1833), 640-45.
No. IV [signed N]. IV (Dec. 31, 1833, supplement), 763-67.
No. V. V (Feb. 1834), 156-61.
No. VI. V (June 1834), 679-85.
No. VII. VI (July 1834), 42-49.
No. VIII. VI (Aug. 1834), 153-58.
No. IX. VI (Sept. 1834), 288-93.
No. X. VI (Oct. 1834), 397-402.
No. XI. VII (May 1835), 519-24.
No. XII. VII (June 1835), 662-68.
No. XIII. VIII (July 1835), 41-45.
No. XIV. VIII (Aug. 1835), 158-65.
No. XV. VIII (Sept. 1835), 277-84.
No. XVI [Apollinaris]. X (July 1836), 35-41.
No. XVII. X (Aug. 1836), 148-54.
No. XVIII. X (Sept. 1836), 281-87.
No. XIX. XI (April 1837), 398-405.
No. XX. XI (May 1837), 517-22.
Copy of *British Magazine* at B.O. with corrections in N's hand in nos. I, II, V, IX, XIV, XVI, and XVII.

Later published as *The Church of the Fathers.* See **A10a.**
Then in *H.S.*, II, with the exception of No. XVI on Apol-

linaris which was put into "Primitive Christianity," *H.S.*, I.
See **A31a,d,1; A31a,c,k.**

B3e "Lyra apostolica, no. I," III (June 1, 1833), 656-57.
1. The course of truth (When royal truth, released from his earth-throes).
2. The Greek Fathers (Let others hymn thy heathen praise).
3. David numbering the people (If e'er I fall beneath thy rod).
4. The saint and the hero (O aged saint! far off I heard).

B3f "Lyra apostolica, no. II," IV (July 1833), 24-25.
2. The cruel Church (O Mother Church of Rome! why has thy heart).
3. ΠΑΥΛΟΥ ΜΙΜΗΤΗΣ (O Lord! when sin's close-marshalled line).
4. Moses seeing the land (My father's hope! my childhood's dream).
5. The pains of memory (What time my heart unfolded its fresh leaves).

B3g "Lyra apostolica, no. IV," IV (Sept. 1, 1833), 265-67.
1. England (Tyre of the West, and glorying in the name).
2. Uzzah and Obededom (The ark of God has hidden strength).
3. The beasts of Ephesus (How long, O Lord of grace!).
   This was published in *Lyra apostolica* under the title "Conservatism." See **C33a.**
4. St. Paul in prison (O comrade bold of toil and pain!).

B3h "Lyra apostolica, no. VI," IV (Nov. 1833), 517-18.
1. Autumn (Now is the Autumn of the tree of life).
2. "It is I, be not afraid" (When I sink down in gloom or fear).
3. David and Jonathan (Oh heart of fire! misjudged by wilful man).
4. The penitent and not the righteous (My smile is bright, my glance is free).

B3i "Lyra apostolica, no. VIII," V (Jan. 1, 1834), 35-37.
1. The patient Church (Bide thou thy time).
2. The backwood Church (Wake mother dear, the foes are near).

3. The gathering of the Church (Wherefore shrink, and say, " 'Tis vain).
4. The Church in prayer (Why loiterest within Simon's walls).
5. The prospects of the Church (Christ only, of God's messengers to man).
Note added: Errata in the November number: p. 517, line 6, for "skill" read "still"; last line, for "portrait" read "portent"; p. 518, line 18, for "they" read "these."

B3j "Lyra apostolica, no. IX," V (Feb. 1, 1834), 153-56.
1. Disappointment (Did we but see,).
2. Faith (Lead, kindly light). See **A34a**.
3. Confession (Mortal! if e'er thy spirits faint).
5. Peace (Whene'er goes forth Thy solemn word).
Later reprinted in *Lyra apostolica* as "Whene'er goes forth Thy dread command." See **C33a**.

B3k "Lyra apostolica, no. XI," V (April 1834), 431-32.
1. The zeal of Jehu (Ye cannot halve the gospel of God's grace).
3. When mirth is full and free.
4. The world has cycles in its course, when all.
5. I have been honoured and obeyed.

B3l "Lyra apostolica, no. XII," V (May 1834), 544-46.
1. When first earth's rulers welcomed home.
2. There is one only bond in the wide earth.
3. Faint not, and fret not, for threatened foe.
4. Christ's Church was holiest in her youthful days.
5. St. Paul at Melita (Secure in Truth's predictive strength). Later reprinted in *Lyra apostolica* as: "Secure in his prophetic strength." See **C33a**.

B3m "Lyra apostolica, no. XIII," V (June 1834), 672-74.
1. Give any boon for peace.
2. How shall a child of God fulfil.
3. I saw thee once, and nought discerned.
4. Gregorius theologus (Peace-loving man, of humble heart and true).
5. Moses (Moses, the patriot fierce, became).

B3n "Lyra apostolica, no. XIV," VI (July 1834), 31-32.
1. When I am sad, I say.
2. O say not thou art left of God.
3. Each trial has its weight: which whoso bears.
4. The cross (Whene'er across this sinful flesh of mine).
5. Whence is this awe, by stillness spread.

B3o "Lyra apostolica, no. XV," VI (Aug. 1834), 150-52.
1. Poor wanderers, ye are sore distrest.
2. When I would search the truths that in me burn.
3. Athanasius (When shall our northern Church her champion see).
4. Time was, I shrank from what was right.

B3p "Lyra apostolica, no. XVI," VI (Sept. 1, 1834), 271-72.
1. I bear upon my brow the sign.
2. Absolution (O Father, list a sinner's call!).
3. The name of Jesus (I bow at Jesus' name, for 'tis the sign).
4. Dreams (Oh, miserable power).

B3q "Lyra apostolica, no. XVIII," VI (Nov. 1, 1834), 511-12.
1. The call of David (Latest born of Jesse's race).
   Omitted from first and second editions of *Lyra apostolica.*
2. Guardian angels (Are these the tracks of some unearthly friend).
3. Warnings (When heaven sends sorrow).
4. Providences (When I look back upon my former race).

B3r "Lyra apostolica, no. XIX," VI (Dec. 1, 1834), 623-24.
1. The time has been, it seemed a precept plain.
2. How didst thou start, thou holy Baptist, bid.
3. Deep in his meditative bower.
4. *Thou* to wax fierce.

B3s "Lyra apostolica, no. XXII," VII (March 1, 1835), 258-59.
1. The abject (O prophet, tell me not of peace).
2. The distrustful (O Lord and Christ, thy Churches of the south).
3. The restless (Once, as I brooded o'er my guilty state).
4. The ambitious (Unwearied God, before whose face).

B3t "Lyra apostolica, no. XXIII," VII (April 1, 1835), 406-8.
1. The Jews (O piteous race!).
2. The wrath to come (When first God stirred me, and the Church's word).
3. The heathen ('Mid Balak's magic fires).

B3u "Lyra apostolica, no. XXIV," VII (May 1, 1835), 517-19.
3. Weep, mother mine, and veil thine eyes with shame!
5. Say, who is he, in deserts seen.

B3v "Lyra apostolica, no. XXV," VII (June 1, 1835), 660-62.
3. St. Paul (I dreamed that, with a passionate complaint).
4. James and John (Two brothers freely cast their lot).

B3w "Lyra apostolica, no. XXVII," VIII (Aug. 1, 1835), 156-58.
1. Ere yet I left home's youthful shrine.
2. O holy Lord! who with children three.
3. There is not on the earth a soul so base.
4. They do but grope in learning's pedant round.

B3x "Lyra apostolica, no. XXVIII," VIII (Sept. 1, 1835), 275-76.
3. Jeremiah ("Woe's me!" the peaceful prophet cried).
4. Eremites (Two sinners have been grace-endued).

B3y "Lyra apostolica, no. XXIX," VIII (Oct. 1, 1835), 413-15.
1. Dear, sainted friends, I call not you.
2. They are at rest!
3. Weep not for me.
   Originally published in *MP*. See **A52a**.
4. While Moses on the mountain lay.
5. "The Fathers are in dust, yet live to God."

B3z "Lyra apostolica, no. XXXIII," IX (Feb. 1, 1836), 146-48.
1. Memory (My home is now a thousand miles away).
2. The gift of tongues (Once cast with men of language strange).
3. The Latin Church (O that thy creed were sound!).
4. Christmas (How can I keep my Christmas feast).
5. Banished the home of sacred rest.
6. Home (Where'er I roam in this fair English land).

B3aa "Lyra apostolica, no. XXXIV," IX (March 1, 1836), 271-72.
  1. Πολυτλὰς Διὸς Ὀδύσσως (Cease, stranger, cease those piercing notes).
  2. Messina (Why, wedded to the Lord, still yearns my heart).
  3. Taormini (Say, hast thou tracked a traveller's round).
  4. Corfu (I sat beneath an olive's branches gray).
  5. France (France! I will think of thee, as what thou wast).

B3bb "Lyra apostolica, no. XXXV," IX (April 1, 1836), 386-87.
  1. Noah (We are not children of a guilty sire).
  2. Melchizedek (Thrice blest are they who feel their loneliness).
  3. Abraham (The better portion didst thou choose, great heart).
  4. Isaac (Many the guileless years the Patriarch spent).
  5. Israel (O specious sin and Satan's subtle snare).
  6. Joseph (O purest semblance of the eternal Son!).

B3cc "Lyra apostolica, no. XXXVI," IX (May 1, 1836), 510-11.
  1. And wouldst thou reach, rash scholar mine.
  3. Man is permitted much.

B3dd "Lyra apostolica, no. XXXVIII," X (July 1, 1836), 34-35.
  1. In childhood, when with eager eyes.
     Originally published in *MP*. See **A52a**.
  2. Lord, in this dust Thy sovereign voice.
     Originally published in *MP*. See **A52a**.

B3ee "Lyra apostolica, no. XXXIX," X (Aug. 1, 1836), 137-38.
  1. Samaria (O rail not at our brethren of the north).
  2. Deeds not words (Prune thou thy words, the thoughts control).
  3. Whene'er I seek the holy altar's rail.

B3ff "Lyra apostolica, no. XL," X (Sept. 1, 1836), 272-73.
  1. Thy words are good, and freely given.
  3. Do not their souls, who 'neath the altar wait.

  All the poems, **B3c-ff**, with the exception of "O holy Lord! who with children three" (later called "Temptation"), were next published in *Lyra apostolica*. A few were reprinted in *VRS*, and eighty-eight in *V.V.*, 1868. See Noel. "The call of David" was omitted from the first and second editions of *Lyra apostolica.* See **C33a-j.**

B4 *British Review and London Critical Journal*

B4a "Duncan's Travels in North America," XXII (May 1824), 144-67.

B5 *The Catholic Standard*

B5a "Who's to blame?" signed: "Catholicus," 3, 10, 17, 24, 31 March, 7, 14, 21 April 1855.
    Later published as "Who's to blame?" in *D.A.* See **A18a.**

B6 *The Catholic University Gazette*

B6a "On the object of the essays which are to follow," I (June 1, 1854), 3-5.
    Later published as Ch. I: "Introductory," *O.W.* and *H.S.*, III. See **A57a, A31a,b,m.**

B6b The examination at entrance," I (June 1, 1854), 5-7.
    Later published as "Grammar in elementary subjects," *L.U.S.*, and "Elementary studies" ("#1 Grammar"), *Idea.* See **A35a, A33a.**

B6c "The primâ facie idea of a university," I (June 8, 1854), 10-14.
    Later published as Ch. II: "What is a university?" *O.W.* and *H.S.*, III. See **A57a, A31a,b,m.**

B6d "Athens, the fit site of a university," I (June 15, 1854), 18-24.
    Later published as Ch. III: "Site of a university," *O.W.* and *H.S.*, III. See **A57a, A31a,b,m.**

B6e "The entrance examination a trial of accuracy," I (June 22, 1854), 25-32.
    Later published as "Elementary studies" (introductory remarks and "#1 Grammar"), *L.U.S.* and *Idea.* See **A35a, A33a.**

B6f "Athens, considered as a type of a university," I (June 29, 1854), 33-39.

Later published as Ch. IV: "University life: Athens," *O.W.* and *H.S.*, III.   See **A57a, A31a,b,m.**

B6g "Specimens of youthful inaccuracy of mind," I (July 6, 1854), 41-47.
Later published as "Elementary studies" ("#2 Composition"), *L.U.S.* and *Idea.*   See **A35a, A33a.**

B6h "What a university does, and what it does not, consist in," I (July 13, 1854), 50-55.
Later published as Ch. V: "Free trade in knowledge: The sophists," *O.W.* and *H.S.*, III.   See **A57a, A31a,b,m.**

B6i "The communication of knowledge, the life of the medieval universities," I (July 20, 1854), 58-64.
Later published as Ch. XIV: "Supply and demand: The schoolmen," *O.W.* and *H.S.*, III.   See **A57a, A31a,b,m.**

B6j "Objections answered," I (July 27, 1854), 65-72.
Later published as Ch. VI: "Discipline and influence," *O.W.* and *H.S.*, III.   See **A57a, A31a,b,m.**

B6k "Professorial and tutorial systems," I (Aug. 3, 1854), 75-80.
Later published as Ch. XV: "Professors and tutors," *O.W.* and *H.S.*, III.   See **A57a, A31a,b,m.**

B6l "Athenian and imperial schools contrasted," I (Aug. 10, 1854), 82-87.
Later published as Ch. VII: "Athenian schools: Influence," *O.W.* and *H.S.*, III.   See **A57a, A31a,b,m.**

B6m "Macedonian and Roman schools," I (Aug. 17, 1854), 89-95.
Later published as Ch. VIII: "Macedonian and Roman schools: Discipline," *O.W.* and *H.S.*, III. See **A57a, A31a,b,m.**

B6n "Downfall and refuge of ancient civilization," I (Aug. 24, 1854), 97-101.
Later published as Ch. IX: "Downfall and refuge of ancient civilization: The Lombards," *O.W.* and *H.S.*, III.   See **A57a, A31a,b,m.**

B6o "On the formation of a Catholic literature in the English tongue, no. I," I (Aug. 31, 1854), 105-9.

Later published as "English Catholic literature" ("#1 In its relation to religious literature" and "#2 In its relation to science"), *L.U.S.* and *Idea.* See **A35a, A33a.**

B6p "On the formation of a Catholic literature in the English tongue, no. II," I (Sept. 7, 1854), 113-19.

Later published, slightly changed at beginning and end, as "English Catholic literature," ("#3 In its relation to classical literature"), *L.U.S.* and *Idea.* See **A35a, A33a.**

B6q "The tradition of civilization," I (Sept. 14, 1854), 121-27.

Later published as Ch. X: "The tradition of civilization: The isles of the North," *O.W.* and *H.S.*, III. See **A57a, A31a,b,m.**

B6r "On a characteristic of the popes," I (Sept. 21, 1854), 129-34.

Later published as Ch. XI: "A characteristic of the popes: St. Gregory the Great," *O.W.* and *H.S.*, III. See **A57a, A31a, b,m.**

B6s "On the lesson to be gained from the aforesaid characteristic of the popes," I (Sept. 28, 1854), 139-42.

Later published as Ch. XII: "Moral of that characteristic of the popes: Pius the Ninth," *O.W.* and *H.S.*, III. See **A57a, A31a,b,m.**

B6t "The rise of universities," I (Oct. 5, 1854), 146-51.

Later published as Ch. XIII: "Schools of Charlemagne: Paris," *O.W.* and *H.S.*, III. See **A57a, A31a,b,m.**

B6u "Professors and lecturers of the university," I (Oct. 19, 1854), 162-64.

B6v "L'Ecole des Hautes Etudes at Paris," I (Oct. 19, 1854), 165-67.

Later published as Ch. XX: "Universities and seminaries: L'Ecole des Hautes Etudes," *O.W.* and *H.S.*, III. Ten paragraphs added at the beginning. See **A57, A31a,b,m.**

B6w "On the opening of the schools in arts," I (Nov. 2, 1854), 178-80.

B6x "The ancient University of Dublin," I (Nov. 2, 1854), 180-84.

Later published as Ch. XVII: "The ancient University of Dublin," *O.W.* and *H.S.*, III. See **A57a, A31a,b,m.**

B6y "On the place held by the Faculty of Arts in the university course," I (Nov. 16, 1854), 193-200.

Later published as "Christianity and letters," *L.U.S.* and *Idea*. See **A35a, A33a.**

B6z "Abelard, as representing the strength and weakness of university schools," I (Nov. 23, 1854), 202-6.

Later published as Ch. XVI: "The strength and weakness of universities: Abelard," *O.W.* and *H.S.*, III. See **A57a, A31a,b,m.**

B6aa "Colleges the correction of the deficiencies of the university principle," I (Nov. 30, 1854), 210-16.

Later published as Ch. XVIII: "Colleges the corrective of universities: Oxford," *O.W.* and *H.S.*, III. See **A57a, A31a, b,m.**

B6bb "Spanish universities in the fifteenth century," I (Dec. 7, 1854), 218-23.

Later published in *Campaign*, 437-47. See **D11.**

B6cc "Abuses of the collegiate system," I (Dec. 14, 1854), 227-32.

Later published as Ch. XIX: "Abuses of the colleges: Oxford," *O.W.* and *H.S.*, III. See **A57a, A31a,b,m.**

B6dd "On the nascent infidelity of the day," I (Dec. 21, 1854), 236-40, (Dec. 28, 1854), 243-48.

Later published as "A form of infidelity of the day," *L.U.S.* and *Idea*. See **A35a, A33a.**

B6ee "On artificial memory," I (Jan. 11, 1855), 267-68, (Feb. 1, 1855), 323-25.

B6ff "On Latin composition," I (Jan. 18, 1855), 294-96.
Later included in "Elementary studies: Mr. Black's confession of his search after a Latin style," *L.U.S.* and *Idea*. See **A35a, A33a.** See also **D8.**

B6gg "On the distribution of a student's time," I (Feb. 8, 1855), 336-38.

B6hh "On keeping diaries," I (Feb. 15, 1855), 354-57.

B6ii "University life in Athens 1900 years ago," I (Feb. 22, 1855), 369-70. Probably by N.

B6jj "Roman College," I (March 1, 1855), 384-86, (April 5, 1855), 410-16, (June 7, 1855), 442-48, (July 5, 1855), 463-66, (Dec. 6, 1855), 492-96. Probably by N.

B6kk "Latin conversation," I (March 1, 1855), 386-87. Probably by N.

B6ll "On getting up books," I (March 1, 1855), 387-89, (March 8, 1855), 400-402.

B6mm "On castle building," I (March 1, 1855), 389-90.

B6nn "Letter of the rector to the Right Rev. D. Moriarity, D.D., bishop of Antigonia, coadjutor-bishop of Kerry, on the subject of university preaching," I (March 8, 1855), 394-400.
Later included in "University preaching," *L.U.S.* and *Idea*. See **A35a, A33a.**

B6oo "Preaching with or without a book," I (April 5, 1855), 416-19.
Later included in "University preaching," *L.U.S.* and *Idea*. See **A35a, A33a.**

B6pp "Public lectures of the university," I (April 5, 1855), 420-22.
Later included, with some omissions, in "Discipline of mind," *L.U.S.* and *Idea*. See **A35a, A33a.** Reprinted in *Letters and diaries*, XVI, 568-71. See **D9.**

B6qq "The study of geometry," I (May 3, 1855), 430-33.

B6rr "University and King's Colleges in London," I (May 3, 1855), 433-36.

> Later published in *Campaign*. See **D11**.

B6ss "The Gazette," I (Nov. 1, 1855), 480-82.

B6tt "The examination for the East India civil appointments," I (Dec. 6, 1855), 486-99.

B6uu "On the general relations between theology and physical science," II (Jan. 3, 1856), 2-14.

> Lecture begins on p. 3.
>
> Later published as "Christianity and physical science," *L.U.S.* and *Idea*. See **A35a, A33a**.

B6vv "The theory of objections—the university," II (March 6, 1856), 43-48.

B6ww "Oxford University reform," II (June 5, 1856), 84-88, (July 3, 1856), 105-11. Probably by N.

B6xx "[Speech of N] at the distribution of prizes by His Grace the archbishop of Dublin [Cullen] in the medical school," II (Aug. 7, 1856), 115-17.

B7 *The Christian Observer.* Conducted by Members of the Established Church.

B7a "On the study of the mathematics," signed: A, XX (May 1821), 293-95.

> See next entry for subsequent publication.

B7b "Hints to religious students at college," signed: A, XXII (Oct. 1822), 623-26.

> Later reprinted, with **B7a**, as *Two letters addressed to "The Christian Observer,"* with two sentences omitted from the first letter. See **A93a**.

B7c "Letter from the Rev. J. H. Newman upon the Oxford tracts, with remarks upon it," signed: John H. Newman, XXXVII (Feb. 1837), 114-26, (March 1837), 141-45; remarks of editor separated, pp. 145ff.

> Later published as Tract 82 and in *V.M.*, II. See **C53a, C79a, A98a**.

B8 *The Conservative Journal*

B8a "Oxford and Rome," 28 Jan. 1843.

"The following letter has been forwarded to us for publication. It is without any signature; but we daresay some of our Oxford readers will find no difficulty in fixing upon the name of the writer. For ourselves, we give it without comment."

The letter is dated 12 Dec. 1842. In *V.M.*, II, N gives Feb. 1843 as date of publication.

Also published as "Appendix," *Dublin Review*, XIV (Feb. 1843), 271-75. See **B10a**. Then in advertisement of *Dev.* (1st and 2d eds.). See **A25a,b,c.** Lastly as "Retractation of anti-Catholic statements," in *V.M.*, II. See **A98a**.

B9 *The Contemporary Review*

B9a "The development of religious error," signed: John Henry Cardinal Newman, XLVIII (Oct. 1885), 457-69.

Later published as *The development of religious error; On a criticism urged against a Catholic doctrine*; as Head III in *Criticisms urged against certain Catholic doctrines*; in *E.C.P.*, and as Essay III in *S.E.* See **A14a, A58a, A13a, A28a, A87a**.

B10 *The Dublin Review*

B10a "Appendix" (retractation of anti-Catholic statements), XIV (Feb. 1843), 271-75.

Originally published as "Oxford and Rome," *Conservative Journal*, 28 Jan. 1843. See **B8a**.

Later published in advertisement of *Dev.* (1st and 2d eds.) and in *V.M.*, II. See **A25a,b,c, A98a**.

B10b "Lyra innocentium by the author of the Christian year," XX (June 1846), 434-61.

Later published as "John Keble," *Ess.*, II. See **A27a**.

B11 *London Review*

B11a "Greek tragedy—poetry," I (1828), 153-71.

Copy in Opuscula at B.O. with corrections in N's hand.

Later published as "Poetry with reference to Aristotle's *Poetics*," *Ess.*, I. See **A27a**.

B12   *The Month*

B12a   "The dream of Gerontius," signed: J.H.N., II (May 1865), 415-25, (June 1865), 532-44.
Later published separately as *The dream of Gerontius* and in *V.V.* See **A21a, A97a**.

B12b   "Valentine to a little girl," signed: Daleth, II (June 1865), 143.
Later published in *V.V.* See **A97a**.

B12c   "Ecce homo," IV (June 1866), 551-73.
Later published as "An internal argument for Christianity," *D.A.* See **A18a**.

B12d   "The 'Apologia' in France," V (Dec. 1866), 615-27.
English version of the preface to the French edition of *Apo*.

B12e   "Saints of the desert," nos. I, II, III, signed: J.H.N. (except no. II), I (July–Dec. 1864), 334, 450, 534.

B12f   "Saints of the desert," nos. IV, V, VI, VII, signed: J.H.N., II (Jan.-June 1865), 68, 171, 240, 473.

B12g   "Saints of the desert," nos. VIII, IX, signed: J.H.N., III (July–Dec. 1865), 79-80, 370.

B12h   "Saints of the desert," no. X, signed: J.H.N., IV (Jan.-June 1866), 303-4.

B13   *The Morning Chronicle*

B13a   "The Rev. Dr. Newman and the bishop of Norwich," 21 Oct. 1851.
Letters of N to Dr. Hinds on miracles.
Later published as *A correspondence between the Rev. J. H. Newman, D.D. and the bishop of Norwich on the credibility of miracles*, and as a note at the end of 1872 and subsequent editions of *Prepos*. The correspondence also appeared in the *Tablet*, 25 Oct. 1851, and in the *Rambler*, VIII (Dec. 1851), 443-61. See **A12a, A40e, B18a, B16a**.

B14 *The Nineteenth Century*

B14a "On the inspiration of scripture," XV (Feb. 1884), 185-99.
Later included as Head I in *Criticisms urged against
certain Catholic doctrines*; in *E.C.P.*; and as Essay I in *S.E.*
See **A13a, A28a, A87a.** Reprinted in John Henry Newman,
On the inspiration of scripture, edited with an introduction
by J. Derek Holmes and Robert Murray, S.J. (London, etc.:
Geoffrey Chapman, 1967).

B15 *The Quarterly Theological Review*

B15a "Cooper's crisis," I, no. 3 (June 1825), 33-44.

B16 *The Rambler*

B16a "Miracles—Father Newman and the bishop of Norwich,"
VIII (Dec. 1851), 443-61.
Correspondence and comment.
Originally published in the *Morning Chronicle*. See **B13a.**

B16b "The ancient saints. No. I," signed: O, I, n.s. (May 1859),
90-98.
See **B16e.**

B16c "The ancient saints. Chapter II. St. John Chrysostom. The
separation," signed: O, II, n.s. (Nov. 1859), 41-62.
See **B16e.**

B16d "The ancient saints. Chapter IV. St. Chrysostom—The
exile," signed: O, III, n.s. (July 1860), 189-203.
In the table of contents listed as "The ancient saints
No. III."
See **B16e.**

B16e "The ancient saints. Chapter V. St. Chrysostom—the death,"
signed: O, III, n.s. (Sept. 1860), 338-57.
In the table of contents listed as "The ancient saints.
No. IV."
The four articles (**B16b-e**) were later published as "The
last years of St. John Chrysostom," *H.S.*, II. See **A31a,d,l.**

B16f "The mission of the isles of the north," I, n.s. (May 1859), 1-22, (July 1859), 170-85.

> Later published as "Northmen and Normans in England and Ireland," *H.S.*, III. See **A31a,b,m.**

B16g "The text of the Rheims and Douay version of holy scripture," I, n.s. (July 1859), 145-69.

> Later published as "The history of the text of the Rheims and Douay version of holy scripture," *T.T.* See **A90a.**

B16h "On consulting the faithful in matters of doctrine," signed: O, I, Pt. II, n.s. (July 1859), 189-230.

> Later published in abbreviated form in note V of *Arians* (3d ed. and thereafter). See **A2d.** Both texts reproduced in *On consulting the faithful in matters of doctrine by John Henry Newman*, ed. John Coulson (London: Geoffrey Chapman, 1961).

B16i Contemporary events. I, n.s. (May 1859), 117-44.
I. "Education movement in Ireland."
II. A charter to the Catholic University."

B16j Contemporary events. I, n.s. (July 1859), 251-58.
I. "The Catholic University."

B16k Correspondence. I, n.s. (May 1859).
"Temporal prosperity a note of the Church," signed: O.H., 102-5.
"Questions and answers," signed: H.I., 105-9.
"The prospect of war," signed: J.O., 109-13.
"Traditions of history in the schools," signed: J.J., 113-14.

> The four letters are reprinted in *Letters and diaries*, XIX, 527-39. See **D9.**

B16l Correspondence. I, n.s. (July 1859).
"Temporal prosperity, whether a note of the Church," signed: O.H., 234-36.
"Prosperity, not the price, but a reward of Christian virtue," signed: H., 236-38.
"Lay students in theology," signed: N., 238-41.

The above three letters are reprinted in *Letters and diaries*, XIX, 539-47. See **D9**.

"Designs and prospects of Russia," signed: H.H., 244-47. Possibly by N.

B16m Correspondence. I, n.s. (Sept. 1859).
"Napoleonism not impious," signed: J.O., 378-79.
Reprinted in *Letters and diaries*, XIX, 547-48. See **D9**.

B16n Correspondence. I, n.s. (Sept. 1860).
"Seminaries of the Church," signed: H.O., 398-401.
Reprinted in *Letters and diaries*, XIX, 554-57. See **D9**.

B16o Literary notices, I, n.s. (May 1859).
"*The failure of the queen's colleges and of mixed education in Ireland.* By John Pope Hennessy of the Inner Temple (London, Bryce)," 114-15.
"*Lectures and essays on university subjects.* By John Henry Newman, D.D. (London, Longmans)," 115-16.
"*Complete Latin prosody of Emmanuel Alvarez, S.J.* By James Stewart, M.A. (Dublin, Duffy, 1859), 116.

B16p Literary notices. I, n.s. (Sept. 1859), 391-95, 396. Possibly by N.

B17 *The Record*

B17a "Church reform," signed: "A Churchman," 28 Oct. 1833. Sent from Oxford, 21 Oct. 1833. See **B17e** for subsequent publication.

B17b "Church reform—No. II," signed: "A Churchman," 31 Oct. 1833.
Sent from Oxford, n.d. See **B17e**.

B17c "Church reform—No. III," signed: "A Churchman," 7 Nov. 1833.
See **B17e**.

B17d "Church reform—No. IV," signed: "A Churchman," 11 Nov. 1833.
Sent from Oxford, n.d. See **B17e**.

B17e "Church reform—No. V," signed: "A Churchman," 14 Nov. 1833.

>Sent from Oxford, n.d.

>The five letters (**B17a-e**) were later published as *Five letters on Church reform.* See **A30a**.

B18 *The Tablet*

B18a "Very Rev. Dr. Newman and the bishop of Norwich," XII (25 Oct. 1851), 65.

>Originally published in the *Morning Chronicle.* See **B13a**.

B18b "Catholic intelligence. University education. Discourse I. Delivered at the Rotunda on Monday, May 10, 1852, by the Very Rev. J. H. Newman, D.D.; president of the Catholic University of Ireland," XIII (15 May, 1852), 307-9.

>See **A17a**.

B19 *The Times*

B19a "The Tamworth reading room: Letters on an address delivered by Sir Robert Peel, Bart. M.P., on the establishment of a reading room at Tamworth," signed: Catholicus, 5, 9, 10, 12, 20, 22, 26 Feb. 1841.

>Later published as *The Tamworth reading room* and in *D.A.* See **A89a, A18a**.

B20 *The Undergraduate*

B20a No. I (Monday, Feb. 8, 1819), signed: N., 8 pp.
>See **C84a**.

B21 *The Weekly Register*

B21a "The Catholic University. Its defense and recommendation," 23, 30 Jan., 6, 13 Feb., 6, 13 March 1858.

>Later published with some omissions in *Campaign*, pp. 345-81, and in *Letters and diaries*, XVIII, 565-83. See **D11, D9**.

C

Works Edited, Translated, or with Contributions by John Henry Newman

Note: The entries in this section have been arranged alphabetically according to general headings; the number assigned the general headings are inclusive of the items that follow, e.g., **C10-16.** Fathers of the Church. After the general headings, items are listed in alphabetical order except for the entries of Athanasius, *Encyclopaedia metropolitana*, Fathers of the Church, Claude Fleury, *Lyra apostolica*, and Tracts for the Times, which are more suitably listed chronologically.

C1-2   Andrewes, Lancelot, bishop of Wincester, 1555–1626

C1a   The devotions of Bishop Andrewes, translated from the Greek and arranged anew. [Advertisement signed: J. H. N.] Oxford: John Henry Parker, 1842.

    vi, 170 pp.

    Originally published as *The Greek devotions of Bishop Andrews* [sic], *translated and arranged*, Tract 88. See **C82a, C53a.**

C1b   The devotions of Bishop Andrewes, translated from the Greek and arranged anew. [Advertisement signed: J. H. N.] Oxford: John Henry Parker, 1842.

    vi, 169 pp.

    Bound in one volume with *The private devotions of Dr. Lancelot Andrewes*, trans. from the Latin (J. M. Neale) (Oxford: John Henry Parker, 1844).

C1c   The devotions of Bishop Andrewes, translated from the Greek and arranged anew. New York: Stanford and Swords, 1853.

    viii, (9) 154 pp.

    Bound with Thomas Wilson, Bp. of Sodor and Man, *Sacra privata* (New York, 1853).

C1d   The devotions of Bishop Andrewes translated from the Greek and arranged anew. A new edition. [Advertisement signed:

J. H. N.] Oxford: John Henry Parker and James Parker, 1865.
viii, 168 pp.

> Part II has title: *The private devotions of Dr. Lancelot Andrewes, sometime lord bishop of Winchester*, translated from the Latin (by J. M. Neale).

C2a   The private devotions of Dr. Lancelot Andrewes. New edition. Oxford: J. Parker, 1873.
vii, 174 pp.

C2b   The private devotions of Lancelot Andrewes. A new edition. Edited and revised from the translations of John Henry Newman and J. M. Neale by E. Venables, etc. London: Suttaby & Co., 1883.
xix, 240 pp.

C2c   The private devotions of Lancelot Andrewes. A new edition. Edited and revised from the translations of John Henry Newman and J. M. Neale by E. Venables, etc. London: Suttaby & Co., 1885.
xx, 285 pp.

C3   Athanasius, St., Patriarch of Alexandria, d. 373

C3a   Select treatises of St. Athanasius in controversy with the Arians. Freely translated by John Henry Cardinal Newman. 2 vols. Second edition. London: Pickering and Co., 1881.
xii, 426 pp.; vi, 476 pp.

> Vol. II is an appendix of illustrations.
> Originally published as *Select treatises. . . .* in Library of the Fathers. See **C14a, C16a.**
> Both the translation and the notes were considerably revised in this edition.

C3b   Select treatises of St. Athanasius in controversy with the Arians. Freely translated, with an appendix, by John Henry Cardinal Newman, Honorary Fellow of Trinity College, Oxford, and late Fellow of Oriel. 2 vols. Fourth edition. London and New York: Longmans, Green, and Co., 1888.
xii, 428 pp.; viii, 476 pp.

> Vol. II is an appendix of illustrations.

The advertisement in this edition listed as "Advertisement to the third edition," dated Feb. 2, 1881, is, with a few small changes, the same as that of the second edition. No copy marked "third edition" has been located.

A postscript was added to the fourth edition.

C3c Select treatises of St. Athanasius in controversy with the Arians. Freely translated, with an appendix, by John Henry Cardinal Newman, Honorary Fellow of Trinity College, Oxford, and late Fellow of Oriel. 2 vols. Fifth edition. London and New York: Longmans, Green, and Co., 1890.

xii, 428 pp.; viii, 476 pp.

Vol. II is an appendix of illustrations.

C4 Bible. English. Selections

C4a Maxims of the kingdom of heaven. [Advertisement signed: J. H. N.] London: Burns and Lambert, 1860.

viii, 77 pp.

C4b Maxims of the kingdom of heaven. Second edition, enlarged and re-arranged for meditation and reference. [Note to the first edition signed: 1860 J. H. N.] London: R. Washbourne, 1873.

viii, 541 pp.

C5 Bible. New Testament

C5a Catena aurea. Commentary on the Four Gospels, collected out of the works of the Fathers by S. Thomas Aquinas. Vol. I. St. Matthew. Part I. [Preface signed: J. H. N.] Oxford: John Henry Parker; London: J. G. F. and J. Rivington, 1841.

xiii, 402 pp.

Last paragraph of preface reads: "It only remains to add that the editors are indebted for the translation of St. Matthew, as well as for the above introductory remarks, to the Rev. Mark Pattison, M.A. Fellow of Lincoln College."

C6 Bowden, John William, 1798–1844

C6a Thoughts on the work of the six days of creation. [Preface signed: J. H. N.] Oxford: J. H. Parker, 1845.

viii, 130 (1) pp.

C7 *British Critic. Quarterly Theological Review and Ecclesiastical Record*

C7a XXIV (July 1838) to XXIX (April 1841) edited by N.

"I could not the other day at the moment say whether my Editorship of the B. C. [*British Critic*] ended in April / 41 or in July. But now it is clear that it ended in April." See rest of the letter to W. J. Copeland, 19 Aug. 1875, *Letters and Diaries*, XXVII, 345.

C8 Education

C8a "Cathedra sempiterna." Pp. 82-84 in Omaggio catholico in varie lingue ai principi degli apostoli Pietro e Paolo nel XVIII centenario dal loro martirio. [Ed. Valerian Cardella, S.J.] Roma: E. Linimberghi, 1867.

Put together from passages taken from Discourse I, *Discourses on the scope and nature of university education*, pp. 22, 25-28. See **A17a,b**.

Later printed in *Campaign*, pp. 211-14. See **D11**.

C9 *Encyclopaedia metropolitana*

C9a "Logic," by Richard Whatley, 1823, *in* Encyclopaedia metropolitana; or system of universal knowledge: on a methodical plan projected by Samuel Taylor Coleridge. Edited by the Rev. Edward Smedley . . . the Rev. Hugh James Rose . . . and the Rev. Henry John Rose. . . . London: B. Fellowes, F. & J. Rivington et al., 1817–45. Second edition revised. London: John Joseph Griffin & Co.; Glasgow: Richard Griffin & Co., 1850, 1852, 1853.

For N's part in this, see letter of N to Monsell, 10 Oct. 1852, *Letters and diaries*, XV, 175-79.

Later published in *Elements of logic, comprising the substance of the article in the* Encyclopaedia metropolitana: *with additions, &c.* (London: Printed for J. Mawman, 1826), xxxii, 340 pp. Other editions of the latter appeared in 1827, 1831, 1836, 1840, 1844, 1848.

C9b "Marcus Tullius Cicero," 1824, *in* Encyclopaedia metropolitana. Third Division: History and Biography.

Corrections were made in this article for the 1852 small edition of the *Encyclopaedia*.

Later published in *H.S.*, I, with half-title page: "Personal and literary character of Cicero." See **A31a,c,k.**

C9c "The life of Apollonius Tyanaeus; with a comparison of the miracles of scripture and those related elsewhere, as regards their respective object, nature, and evidence," 1826, *in* Encyclopaedia metropolitana. Third Division: History and Biography.

Later published separately as a reprint. See **A49a.** Then published as "Apollonius of Tyana," *H.S.*, I. See **A31a,c,k.** The part on miracles was put into *Mir.* See **92a.**

C10-16 Fathers of the Church

C10a A Library of the Fathers of the Holy Catholic Church, anterior to the division of the East and the West. Translated by members of the English Church. Edited by E. B. Pusey, J. H. Newman, J. Keble, and C. Marriott. Oxford: John Henry Parker; London: J. G. F. & J. Rivington, 1838–85.

Of the following, N translated *Select Treatises of S. Athanasius* and edited the others.

C11a The catechetical lectures of S. Cyril, archbishop of Jerusalem, translated with notes and indices. [Preface signed: J.H.N.] Oxford: John Henry Parker; London: J. G. F. and J. Rivington, 1838. [Library of the Fathers.]

xxxviii, 312 pp.

Copy at B.O. inscribed: "John H. Newman / Oriel College / Nov. 2, 1838." Corrections in N's hand.

C12a The treatises of S. Caecilius Cyprian, bishop of Carthage, and martyr. Translated with notes and indices. [Preface signed: J.H.N.] Oxford: John Henry Parker; London: J. G. F. & J. Rivington, 1839. [Library of the Fathers.]

xxvi, 318 pp.

Reprinted in 1840, 1842, 1846, 1876 (Library of the Fathers).

C13a Commentary on the epistle to the Galatians, and homilies on the epistle to the Ephesians, of S. John Chrysostom, arch-

bishop of Constantinople, translated with notes and indices. [Preface signed: J.H.N.] Oxford: John Henry Parker; London: J. G. F. and J. Rivington, 1840. [Library of the Fathers.]
    xv, 401 (1) pp.

C14a Select treatises of S. Athanasius, archbishop of Alexandria, in controversy with the Arians, translated, with notes and indices. [Advertisement signed: J. H. N. On spine: Part I.] Oxford: John Henry Parker; London: J. G. F. and J. Rivington, 1842. [Library of the Fathers.]
    vi, 280 pp.
    Reprinted in 1877 (Library of the Fathers). See note on **C16a** for N's republication.

C15a Historical tracts of S. Athanasius, archbishop of Alexandria, translated with notes and indices. [Preface signed: J. H. N.] Oxford: John Henry Parker; London: J. G. F. and J. Rivington, 1843. [Library of the Fathers.]
    xxviii, 321 pp.
    Notes are also by N.
    Reprinted in 1873 (Library of the Fathers).

C16a Select treatises of S. Athanasius, archbishop of Alexandria, in controversy with the Arians, translated with notes and indices. [Note at the beginning: "The Preliminary Matter is unavoidably postponed. J. H. N. *Dec.* 6, 1844." On spine: Part II.] Oxford: John Henry Parker; London: J. G. F. and J. Rivington, 1844. [Library of the Fathers.]
    xiv (2), 596 pp.
    Reprinted in 1869 (Library of the Fathers).
    C14a and **C16a** were republished in a considerably revised edition as *Select treatises of St. Athanasius in controversy with the Arians*, 2 vols., 1881. See **C3a**.

C17-19 Fleury, Claude, 1640–1723

C17a The ecclesiastical history of M. L'Abbé Fleury, from the second ecumenical council to the end of the fourth century. Translated with notes, and an essay on the miracles of the period. [Advertisement signed: J.H.N.] Oxford: John Henry Parker; London: Rivingtons, 1842.

ccxx, 400 pp.

Contains "Essay on the miracles," pp. xi-ccxvi, by N. This essay was published separately as *An essay on the miracles recorded in the ecclesiastical history of the early ages*, 1843. See **A26a**. It was later included in *Mir*. See **A92a**.

C18a The ecclesiastical history of M. L'Abbé Fleury, from A.D. 400 to A.D. 429. Translated with notes. [Advertisement signed: J. H. N.] Oxford: John Henry Parker; London: J. G. F. and J. Rivington, 1843.

viii, 468 pp.

C19a The ecclesiastical history of M. L'Abbé Fleury, from A.D. 429 to A.D. 456. Translated,with notes. [Advertisement signed: J. H. N.] Oxford: John Henry Parker; London: J. G. F. and J. Rivington, 1844.

viii, 471 pp.

C20-21 Froude, Richard Hurrell, 1803–1836

C20a Remains of the late Richard Hurrell Froude, M.A., Fellow of Oriel College, Oxford. [Edited by N and J. Keble.] In two volumes. London: Printed for J. G. and F. Rivington, 1838.

xxii (1), 497 pp.; viii, 423 pp.

"The Preface to Froude's Remains, consisting of 22 pages, is certainly Keble's, not mine, except the portion about 'Romanism' from p[.] ix to p[.] xv. I speak of the Preface to the First Series—The Preface to the Second Series is all Keble's, except a few formal lines at the end, which I think are mine" (*Letters and diaries*, XXXI, p. 87* and note 2).

Copy at B.O. with note on flyleaf: "Published St. Matthew's day 1838. So many relics of a frail love lost / So many tokens dear / of endless love begun / J.H.N."

C21a Remains of the late Richard Hurrell Froude, M.A., Fellow of Oriel College, Oxford. Part the second. In two volumes. Derby: Printed by Henry Mozley and Sons, and sold by J. G. & F. Rivington, London, 1839.

xlvii (3), 410 pp.; xv, 633 (1) pp.

C22 Hutton, Arthur Wollaston, 1848–1912

C22a The Anglican ministry. Its nature and value in relation to the Catholic priesthood. With a preface by His Eminence Cardinal Newman, founder of the English Oratory. London: C. Kegan Paul & Co., 1879.
xx, 550 pp.

C23-30 Hymns

C23a A collection of hymns in use at the Oratory of St. Philip Neri, at Birmingham. [Anon.] Birmingham: Lander, Powell & Co., 1850.
164 pp.

C24a Hymni ecclesiae, e breviario Parisiensi. [Preface signed: J. H. N.] Oxonii: Apud J. H. Parker, 1838.
xxiv, 203 pp.

C25a Hymni ecclesiae, excerpti e breviariis Romano, Sarisburiensi, Eboracensi, et aliunde. [Preface signed: J. H. N.] Oxonii: J. H. Parker, 1838.
xii, 163 pp.

C26a Hymni ecclesiae. Pars I e breviario Parisiensi. Pars II e breviariis Romano, Sarisburiensi, Eboracensi et aliunde. [Preface signed: J. H. N.] Londini: apud Alexandrum Macmillan, 1865.
xiv, 406 pp.

C27a Hymns by John Henry Newman. New York: E. P. Dutton & Company, 1885.
xx, 21-282 pp.

C28a Hymns for the use of the Birmingham Oratory. [Anon.] Dublin: James Duffy, 1854.
127 pp.
Eighty-two hymns, ten by Newman, two of which are translations from the Roman breviary and eight from *VRS*. The rest are translations of Latin hymns by N's fellow Oratorian, Father Edward Caswall. See Noel.

C28b Hymns for the use of the Birmingham Oratory. [Anon.] Birmingham: Printed by W. Hodgetts, 1862.

82 hymns plus appendixes and index—113 items, total.

C28c Hymns for the use of the Birmingham Oratory. [Anon.] London: Basil Montagu Pickering, 1875.

82 hymns plus appendixes and index—113 items, total.

C28d Hymns for the use of the Birmingham Oratory. [Anon.] London: Basil Montagu Pickering, 1888.

82 hymns plus appendixes and index—149 items, total.

C29a Hymn tunes of the oratory. Accompaniments. [Anon.] Birmingham, 1860.

C30a Hymn tunes of the oratory. Voice. [Anon.] Birmingham, 1860.

C31-32 Lives of Saints

C31a Lives of the English Saints. 14 vols. London: James Toovey, 1844-1845.

"After the two first numbers, I retired from the Editorship." Also letter of N: "I am not Editor. . . . I did edit the two first numbers. I was responsible for them, in the way in which an Editor is responsible" (*Apo.*, p. 211).

James Toovey succeeded N as editor after the first two numbers. Thirty-three lives were completed.

For the series as N originally projected it, see Note D of *Apo.*

For the lives, including biographical sketches of the authors, see *The Lives of the English Saints*, ed. A. W. Hutton, 6 vols. (London, 1900-1901; Philadelphia, 1901).

No. 1. The Cistercian Saints of England. St. Stephen, abbot [St. Stephen Harding]. [J. D. Dalgairns.]

No. 2. The family of St. Richard the Saxon. St. Richard king, St. Willibald, bishop, St. Walburga, virgin abbess, and St. Winibald, abbot. [Thomas Meyrick.]

No. 4. Hermit Saints. This contains seven lives:

I. St. Gundleus. [J. H. Newman.]

II. St. Helier. [J. D. Dalgairns.]

III. St. Herbert. [J. Barrow.]

IV. St. Edelwald. [J. H. Newman.]

V. St. Bettelin. [The prose by J. H. Newman, the verse by J. D. Dalgairns.]
VI. St. Neot. [J. A. Froude.]
VII. St. Bartholomew. [J. D. Dalgairns.]

C32a Lives of the English Saints. Hermit Saints. London: James Toovey, 1844.

The following are by N:

A legend of St. Gundleus, hermit in Wales, about A.D. 500. pp. 1-8.

A legend of St. Edelwald, hermit at Farne, A.D. 700. pp. 49-56.

A legend of St. Bettelin, hermit, and patron of Stafford, towards A.D. 800. [Prose by N; verse by J. D. Dalgairns.] pp. 57-72.

"The few lines of Advertisement to 'Hermit Saints' is mine" (*Letters and diaries*, XXIV, 328).

C33 *Lyra apostolica*

C33a Lyra apostolica. Derby: Henry Mozley and Sons; London: J. G. and F. Rivington, 1836.

[viii], 226(1) pp. and 7 pages of index not numbered.

Poems by: J. W. Bowden, R. H. Froude, J. Keble, J. H. Newman, R. I. Wilberforce, and I. Williams, subscribed respectively α, β, γ, δ, ε, ς.

Originally published as "Lyra apostolica," in the *British Magazine*, III (June 1, 1833), 656, to X (Sept. 1, 1836), 273. For N's contributions see **B3e-ff**.

Twenty-six of N's poems in *Lyra apostolica* were reprinted in *VRS*, eighty-eight (including "The Call of David" added to the third edition) were reprinted in the first edition of *V.V.*, four more in the appendix to the latter, and four in the 1874 edition. See **A96a, A97a, A97e**. The following poems were not reprinted in *V.V.*: "Rome," "Conservatism," "The cruel Church," "Israel," "Science" (There is one only bond in the wide earth), "The desert" ("The Eremites"), "The backward Church," "Protestantism" (Weep, mother mine), "Athanasius," and "The Eucharist" (Whene'er I seek the holy altar's rail).

N was the original editor and owner of the volume. In 1845 or 1846 he gave the ownership to John Keble. Upon Keble's death in 1866, N and Keble's nephew, Thomas Keble, Jr., became involved in a dispute about the copyright. See *Letters and diaries*, XXII, 264-65, 286-87. It was finally settled with the help of H. P. Liddon. See *Letters and diaries*, XXIV, 112-13, 119-20, XXVIII, 429-30, XXIX, 6-7. In 1881 N transferred the copyright to Keble College. See *Letters and diaries*, XXIX, 347-48, 358. Prior to this, N issued a "new edition" in 1879. See **C33j**.

C33b Lyra apostolica. Second edition. Derby: Henry Mozley and Sons; Oxford: Parker; London: J. G. & F. Rivington, 1837. [viii] , 238(1) pp. and 7 pages of index not numbered.

C33c Lyra apostolica. Third edition. Derby: Henry Mozley and Sons; Oxford: Parker; London: J. G. and F. Rivington, 1838. [viii] , 243 pp. and 7 pages of index not numbered.
Two poems added: "The call of David" by J. H. N. and "The winter thrush" by Keble, originally published in *British Magazine.*

C33d Lyra apostolica. Fourth edition. Derby: Henry Mozley and Sons; Oxford: Parker; London: J. G. & F. Rivington, 1840. [viii] , 243 pp. and 7 pages of index not numbered.

C33e Lyra apostolica. Sixth edition. Derby: H. Mozley & Sons, 1843.
[viii] , 243 pp. and 7 pages of index not numbered.

C33f Lyra apostolica. First American, from the fifth edition. New York: D. Appleton & Co.; Philadelphia: Geo. S. Appleton, 1844.

C33g Lyra apostolica. Seventh edition. Derby: Henry Mozley & Sons, 1845.
[viii] , 243 pp. and 7 pages of index not numbered.

C33h Lyra apostolica. Ninth edition. London: John and Charles Mozley, F. and J. Rivington; Oxford: J. H. Parker, 1849.
[viii] , 243 pp. and 7 pages of index not numbered.

C33i Lyra apostolica. Thirteenth edition. London: John & Charles Mozley, J. and F. H. Rivington; Oxford: J. H. Parker, 1864. [viii] , 243 pp. and 7 pages of index not numbered.

C33j Lyra apostolica. [Postscript signed: J.H.N. added to the advertisement.] New edition. London, Oxford and Cambridge: Rivingtons, 1879.

    xvi, 256 pp.

    N added a postscript to the original advertisement in which he identified the contributors, and made small changes in the texts of his own poems.

C34 Lyrics

C34a Lyrics of light and life: XLIII. Original poems by Dr. John Henry Newman, William Alexander, bp. of Derry, Christina Rossetti. . . . [Edited by F. G. Lee.] London: Basil Montagu Pickering, 1875.

    xi (1), 144 pp.

    Contains "My birthday," pp. 6-10. Written Trinity College, Feb. 21, 1819.

    Originally published in *MP*. See **A52a**. Later published in *V.V.*, 1888. See **A97h**.

C35 Nelson, Robert, 1656–1714

C35a The life of George Bull, D.D., some time Lord Bishop of St. Davids. [Preface signed: J. H. N.] Oxford: John Henry Parker, 1840.

    xvi, 332 pp.

C36 Palmer, William, Fellow of Magdalen, 1811–1879

C36a Notes of a visit to the Russian Church in the years 1840, 1841. Selected and arranged by Cardinal Newman. London: Kegan Paul, Trench & Co., 1882.

    xxiv, 572 pp.

    Reprinted by Longmans, Green, and Co., 1895.

C37 Plautus, Titus Macceius, d. 184 B.C.

C37a Aulularia Plauti. Pueris in scenam prodituris accommodata. [Anon.] London: Gilbert and Rivingtons, 1866.

48 pp.

Copy at B.O. with corrections by F. W. Newman.

A37b Aulularia Plauti with English notices to assist the representation. Cardinal Newman's edition. London: Rivingtons, 1883. 48, 29 pp.

C37c Aulularia Plauti with English notices to assist the representation. Cardinal Newman's edition. London: Rivingtons, 1888. 77 pp.

C38 Pope Pius IX, 1792-1878

C38a Allocution of His Holiness, Pope Pius IX, delivered in secret consistory, April 29, 1848. SS. Domini nostri Pii divina providentia Papae IX. Allocutio habita in consistorio secreto die xxix. April, an. MDCCCXLVIII. [Advertisement signed: J. H. N.] London: James Burns, 1848.

16 pp.

C39-40 Prayers

C39a Prayers for unity. [n.p., n.d.]

36 pp.

"One of my first feelings after the shock my opinions had in 1839 was to pray for unity. I revised these (of R. William's & A. Aclad's, I think.)—meanwhile I had drawn up others, *which I did not like*, but thought dull & heavy—but which I thought wd please the High Church (not movement) party, & obtain their concurrence. When I saw these, I gave up my own. (I think it was so) & then, (*I know*) Pusey, agst my wish, got my consent to print my own, which I had not liked. JHN Sept 17/50."

C40a Prayers for unity and guidance into the truth. [Anon.] London: James Burns, 1841.

16 pp.

"These Prayers were drawn up by me with the hope of inducing High Churchmen, not of the movement party, to join in them. Hence they come from the Prayer Book.

"However, I preferred the other compilation, & did not wish this published—but Pusey, imagining, I suppose, that I in *my heart* liked these, & liking them best himself, got my leave to print them.

"They are for Friday, whereas I was in favor of Thursday, which is the day taken in the other compilation. Sept. 17, 1856. JHN."

C41 *The Rambler*

C41a I, n.s. (May 1859) to I, Pt. II, n.s. (July 1859) edited by N.

C42-44 Sermons

C42a A pastoral for Lent, being a plea for the daily service. Burlington, 1843.

  24 pp.

  Two sermons on daily service, one by N on Heb. 10:25; the other by H. E. N. Manning on Acts 2:46-47.

  Originally published as "The Daily Service," *P.S.*, III. See **A64a.**

  Later published in *P.P.S.*, III. See **A69a.**

C43a Plain sermons, by contributors to the "Tracts for the Times." [John Keble, Isaac Williams, E. B. Pusey, J. H. Newman, Thomas Keble, Sir George Provost, and Robert Francis Wilson; indicated respectively by the letters A, B, C, D, E, F, G in a table at the end of vol. 10.] 10 vols. London: Printed for J. G. F. & J. Rivington, 1839-48.

C44a Plain sermons, by contributors to the "Tracts for the Times," [John Keble, Isaac Williams, E. B. Pusey, J. H. Newman, Thomas Keble, Sir George Provost, and Robert Francis Wilson; indicated respectively by the letters A, B, C, D, E, F, G in a table at the end of vol. 10.] 10 vols. 27th series. Vol. 5. [Anon.] London: Printed for J. G. F. & J. Rivington, 1843.

  iv, 342 pp.

  Later published as *P.P.S.*, VII and VIII. See **A69a.**

C45 Sparrow, Anthony, successively Bishop of Exeter and of Norwich, 1612-1685.

C45a A rationale upon the Book of Common Prayer of the Church of England. A new edition. [Editor's preface signed:

J. H. N.] Oxford: J. H. Parker, 1839.
viii (4), 395 pp.

C45b A rationale upon the Book of Common Prayer of the Church of England. [Preface signed: J. H. N.] Oxford: J. H. Parker, 1843.
xiv, 396 pp.

C46-47 Sutton, Christopher, 1565?-1629

C46a Disce vivere. Learn to live. A new edition. [Preface signed: J. H. N.] Oxford: John Henry Parker, 1839.
xx (6), 438 pp.

C46b Disce vivere. Learn to live. New edition. [Preface signed: J. H. N.] Oxford: J. H. Parker, 1841.
xxiv, 437 pp.

C47a Godly meditations upon the most holy sacrament of the Lord's Supper. With many things appertaining to the due receiving of so great a mystery, and to the right disposing ourselves unto the same. [Preface signed: J. H. N.] A new edition. Oxford: John Henry Parker, 1838.
xxxii, 350 pp.

C47b Godly meditations upon the most Holy Sacrament of the Lord's Supper. A new edition. [Preface signed: J. H. N.] Oxford: John Henry Parker, 1839.
xxxvi, 344 pp.

C47c Godly meditations upon the most Holy Sacrament of the Lord's Supper. A new edition by John Henry Newman. Oxford: J. H. Parker, 1841.
xxxvi, 334 pp.

C47d Godly meditations upon the most Holy Sacrament of the Lord's Supper. New York: D. Appleton & Co., 1841.
xxxii, 335 pp.

C48-51 Terentius, Publius

C48a P. Terentii Andria. In usum puerorum. [Anon.] Londini: Gilbert et Rivington, Impressores, 1870.
46 pp.

C48b Andria Terentii with English notices to assist the representation. Cardinal Newman's edition. London: Rivingtons, 1883.
46, 44 pp.

C48c Andria Terentii in usum puerorum with English notices to assist the representation. Cardinal Newman's edition. London: Rivingtons, 1889.
92 pp.

C49a Prologue to the "Andria" of Terence, written by John Henry Newman (now Cardinal Newman) and sent by him to the Rev. Dr. Nicholas, of Great Ealing, Middlesex, with a view to its being repeated at the performance of that play at his old school, and by his former school-fellows, in June, 1820. Printed for private circulation only, 1882.
7 pp.

C50a [Eunuchus.] Pincerna ex Terentio. In usum puerorum. [Anon.] London: Gilbert and Rivingtons, Printers, 1865.
47 pp.
Expurgated edition of *Eunuchus*, to which N gave the title *Pincerna*, the Cup Bearer.
Copy at B.O. with corrections by F. W. Newman.

C50b [Eunuchus.] Pincerna ex Terentio in usum puerorum. [Anon.] Birmingham: Martin Billing, Son, and Co., 1880.
47 pp.

C50c [Eunuchus.] Pincerna ex Terentio with English notices to assist the representation. Cardinal Newman's edition. London: Rivingtons, 1883.
48, 30 pp.

C50d [Eunuchus.] Pincerna ex Terentio with English notices to assist the representation. Cardinal Newman's edition. London: Rivingtons, 1887.
48, 30 pp.

C51a P. Terentii Phormio. Expurgatus in usum puerorum. [Anon.] 1864.
47 pp.
Copy at B.O. with corrections by F. W. Newman.

C51b Phormio Terentii with English notices to assist the representation. Cardinal Newman's edition. London: Rivingtons, 1883.

47, 22 (2) pp.

C51c Phormio Terentii with English notices to assist the representation. Cardinal Newman's edition. London: Rivingtons, 1889.

76 pp.

C52-83 Tracts for the Times

C52a Tracts for the Times.

Note: N began the tracts in 1833. Turrill was the first publisher and King, the printer. Rivingtons took over in the spring of 1834, probably starting with Tract 30. At the B.O. Archives (D.3.6), N's notation on the tracts reads: "In 1833 the Tracts were only sold at King's & Turille's—In 1834 Rivingtons took over the expenses & sub[scription]." The tracts continued to be sold individually, and also in bound volumes, but the bound volumes sometimes contain different editions of individual tracts. Advertisements to vols. I, II, III were written by N. Only the notes in brackets, not the translations, of the *Records of the Church* are N's. Editions checked are listed after each volume.

C53a Tracts for the Times. By members of the University of Oxford. London: Printed for J. G. & F. Rivington, & J. H. Parker, Oxford. 6 vols. 1834-41.

Vol. I for 1833-34. Tracts 1-46 and Records of the Church I-XVIII. 1834, 1838 (new ed.), 1839.

Vol. II for 1834-35. Tracts 47-66 and Records of the Church XIX-XXV. 1836, 1840.

Vol. II, Part II for 1834-35. Tracts 67-70. 1842 (4th ed.).

Vol. III for 1835-36. Advertisement, note to advertisement, and Tracts 71-76. In the table of contents to vol. IV, the preface, title page, and contents to vol. III are listed as Tract 77. However, the "Note to advertisement," containing Pusey's "An earnest remonstrance to the author of the pope's letter" is considered to be

Tract 77. 1836, 1837 (2d ed.), 1840 (new ed.).
Vol. IV for 1836–37. Tracts 78-82. 1838.
Vol. V for 1838–40. Tracts 83-88. 1840.
Vol. VI. Tracts 89-90 (title page missing).
The Tracts by N are given in the following entries. See **C54a-83k.**

C54a No. 1 (*Ad clerum*). Thoughts on the ministerial commission, respectfully addressed to the clergy.
4 pp.

C55a No. 2. The Catholic Church.
4 pp.

C56a No. 3. Thoughts respectfully addressed to the clergy on alterations in the liturgy. The burial service. The principle of unity.
8 pp.

C57a No. 6 (*Ad populum*). The present obligation of primitive practice. A sin of the Church.
4 pp.

C58a No. 7. The episcopal Church apostolical.
4 pp.

C59a No. 8. The gospel a law of liberty. Church reform.
4 pp.

C60a No. 10. Heads of a week-day lecture, delivered to a country congregation in ____shire.
6 pp.

C61a No. 11 (*Ad scholas*). The visible Church. (In *Letters to a friend*). Letters I and II.
8 pp.

C62a No. 15. On the apostolical succession in the English Church.
11 pp.
W. Palmer, revised and completed by N.

C63a No. 19. On arguing concerning the apostolical succession. On reluctance to confess the apostolical succession.
4 pp.

C64a No. 20.(*Ad scholas*). The visible Church. Letters to a friend. No. III.

4 pp.

C65a No. 21 (*Ad populum*). Mortification of the flesh a scripture duty.

4 pp.

C66a No. 31 (*Ad clerum*). The reformed Church.

4 pp.

C67a No. 33 (*Ad scholas*). Primitive episcopacy.

7 pp.

C68a No. 34 (*Ad scholas*). Rites and customs of the Church.

8 pp.

C69a No. 38 (*Ad scholas*). Via media. No. I.

12 pp.

Later published in *V.M.*, II. See **A98a**.

C70a No. 41 (*Ad scholas*). Via media. No. II.

12 pp.

Later published in *V.M.*, II. See **A98a**.

C71a No. 45 (*Ad clerum*). The grounds of our faith.

6 pp.

C72a No. 47 (*Ad clerum*). The visible Church. Letter IV.

4 pp.

C73a No. 71 (*Ad clerum*). On the controversy with the Romanists. (*Against Romanism.*—No. 1.)

35 pp.

Later published as "On the mode of conducting the controversy with Rome," *V.M.*, II. See **A98a**.

C74a No. 73 (*Ad scholas*). On the introduction of rationalistic principles into religion.

56 pp.

Later published as "On the introduction of rationalistic principles into revealed religion," *Ess.*, I. See **A27a**.

C75a No. 74 (*Ad populum*). Catena patrum. No. I. Testimony of

writers in the later English Church to the doctrine of the apostolical succession.
56 pp.

C76a   No. 75 (*Ad clerum*). On the Roman breviary as embodying the substance of the devotional services of the Church Catholic.
207 pp.

C77a   No. 76 (*Ad populum*). Catena patrum. No. II. Testimony of writers in the later English Church to the doctrine of baptismal regeneration.
56 pp.

C78a   No. 79 (*Ad clerum*). On purgatory. (*Against Romanism.—* No. 3.)
61 pp.

C79a   No. 82. Letter to a magazine on the subject of Dr. Pusey's Tract on baptism. [Part of preface to vol. IV of the Tracts.]
37 pp.
Originally published as "Letter from Rev. J. H. Newman upon the Oxford tracts, with remarks upon it," *Christian Observer*, XXXVII (Feb.–March 1837), 114-26, 141-45. See **B7c**.
Later published as "Letter addressed to a magazine on behalf of Dr. Pusey's tracts on holy baptism and of other Tracts for the Times," *V.M.*, II. See **A98a**.

C80a   No. 83. Advent sermons on Antichrist.
54 pp.
Sermon I. The times of Antichrist.
Sermon II. The religion of Antichrist.
Sermon III. The city of Antichrist.
Sermon IV. The persecution of Antichrist.
Later published as "The patristical idea of Antichrist," *D.A.* See **A18a**.

C81a   No. 85. Lectures on the scripture proof of the doctrines of the Church. Part I.
115 pp.
Lecture I. Difficulties in the scripture proof of the doctrines of the Church.

Lecture II. The difficulties of Latitudinarianism.

Lecture III. On the general structure of the Bible as a record of faith.

Lecture IV. Mode in which facts of history are contained in scripture.

Lecture V. The impression conveyed by the statement of facts and doctrines in scripture.

Lecture VI. External difficulties of the Canon and the Catholic Creed, compared.

Lecture VII. Internal difficulties of the Canon and the Catholic Creed compared.

Lecture VIII. Difficulties of Jewish and Christian faith compared.

Later published as "Holy scripture in its relation to the Catholic Creed," *D.A.* See **A18a.**

C82a No. 88. The Greek devotions of Bishop Andrews [*sic*], translated and arranged.

96 pp.

Later published as *The devotions of Bishop Andrewes, translated from the Greek and arranged anew*, 1842. See **C1a,b,c,d.**

C83a No. 90. Remarks on certain passages in the Thirty-nine Articles. London: Printed for J. G. F. & J. Rivington, 1841.

83 pp.

C83b No. 90. Remarks on certain passages in the Thirty-nine Articles. Second edition. London: Printed for J. G. F. & J. Rivington, 1841.

83 pp.

The corrections in the second edition are put in brackets.

C83c No. 90. Remarks on certain passages in the Thirty-nine Articles. Fourth edition. London: Printed for J. G. F. & J. Rivington, 1842.

83 pp.

Later published in *V.M.*, II (see **A98a**) and separately in the following editions.

C83d Tracts for the Times, no. 90. Reprinted with introduction and notes by the Rev. James Joseph Frew. [Fourth edition.] London: Hope and Company, 1855.

xii, 82 pp.

This seems to have been a pirated edition. See *Letters and diaries*, XVI, 454, n. 2.

C83e Tract XC. On certain passages in the XXXIX Articles. By the Rev. J. H. Newman, B.D., 1841. With a historical preface by the Rev. E. B. Pusey, D.D., and Catholic subscription to the XXXIX Articles considered in reference to Tract XC by the Rev. John Keble, M.A. [Reprinted from fourth edition.] Sold by John Henry and James Parker, Oxford, and Rivingtons, London, Oxford, and Cambridge, 1865.

xxviii, 87 pp.; 26 pp.

C83f Remarks on certain passages in the Thirty-nine Articles. [Reprinted from second English edition.] New York: H. B. Durand, 1865.

134 pp.

C83g Tract XC. On certain passages in the XXXIX Articles. By the Rev. J. H. Newman, B.D., 1841. With a historical preface by the Rev. E. B. Pusey, D.D., and Catholic subscription to the XXXIX Articles considered in reference to Tract XC. By the Rev. John Keble, M.A. Revised edition of the preface. Fourth thousand. [Stereotyped edition, reprinted (with the author's permission) from the fourth edition.] Sold by John Henry and James Parker, Oxford, and Rivington, London, Oxford, and Cambridge, 1866.

xliii, 87; 26 pp.

C83h Tract XC. On certain passages in the XXXIX Articles. By the Rev. J. H. Newman, B.D., 1841. With a historical preface by the Rev. E. B. Pusey, D.D., and Catholic subscription to the XXXIX Articles considered in reference to Tract XC. By the Rev. John Keble, M.A. Revised edition of the preface. Sold by John Henry and James Parker, Oxford and Rivingtons, London, and Cambridge, 1870.

xliii, 87; 26 pp.

C83i Tract XC. On certain passages in the XXXIX Articles. By the Rev. J. H. Newman, B.D., 1841. With a historical preface by the Rev. E. B. Pusey, D.D., and Catholic subscription to the XXXIX Articles considered in reference to Tract XC. By the Rev. John Keble, M.A. Sixth thousand. [Reprinted from the fourth edition.] Sold by James Parker & Co., Oxford; Rivingtons, London, 1881.

xliii, 87; 26 pp.

C83j Tract XC. On certain passages in the XXXIX Articles. By the Rev. J. H. Newman, B.D., 1841. With a historical preface by the Rev. E. B. Pusey, D.D., and Catholic subscription to the XXXIX Articles considered in reference to Tract XC. By the Rev. John Keble, M.A. Revised edition of the preface. Seventh thousand. Sold by James Parker & Co., Oxford and Rivingtons, London, 1882.

xliii, 87; 26 pp.

C83k Tract XC. On certain passages in the XXXIX Articles. By the Rev. J. H. Newman, B.D., 1841. With a historical preface by the Rev. E. B. Pusey, D.D., and Catholic subscription to the XXXIX Articles considered in reference to Tract XC. By the Rev. John Keble, M.A. Revised edition of the preface. London: Walter Smith and Innes (late Mozley), 1888.

xliii, 87; 26 pp.

C84 *The Undergraduate*

C84a Magazine started and conducted by N. and John William Bowden. Six numbers, Feb. and March 1819.

Copies at the B.O. with N's designations:

No. 1. Monday, Feb. 8th, 1819—1-8. By N.

No. 2. Monday, Feb. 15th, 1819. By Bowden.

No. 3. Monday, Feb. 22nd, 1819. By Bowden.

No. 4. Monday, March 1st, 1819. "I do not know who contributed to this paper. JHN."

No. 5. Missing.

No. 6. Saturday, March 20th, 1819. "I do not know who wrote this letter."

C85 Wells, Edward, 1667–1727

C85a The rich man's duty to contribute liberally to the building, rebuilding, repairing, beautifying, and adorning of churches. Rev. Edward Wells. [Preface signed: J. H. N.] Oxford: John Henry Parker, 1840.

> xvi, 205 pp.

> Together with *Journal of William Downing of Stratford, the Parliamentary visitor appointed under a warrant from the earl of Manchester, for demolishing the . . . pictures and ornaments of churches, etc. within the county of Suffolk in the years 1643, 1644,* 37 pp.

C86 Wilberforce, Henry William, 1807–1874

C86a The Church and the empires: historical periods, by. . . . Preceded by a memoir of the author by J. H. Newman. London: H. S. King & Co., 1874.

> 320 pp.

> Memoir, pp. 1-16, dated July 14, 1873.

C87 Wilson, Thomas, Bishop of Sodor and Man, 1663–1755

C87a Sacra privata. The private meditations, devotions, and prayers of Right Rev. T. Wilson. . . . Reprinted entire. [Preface signed: J. H. N.] Oxford: J. H. Parker, 1840.

> xvi, 413 pp.

C87b Sacra privata: The private meditations, devotions, and prayers of the Rev. Thomas Wilson. With a preface by J. H. Newman. . . . Reprinted entire. New York: D. Appleton and Company, 1841.

> 338 pp.

Addendum

C88 Tyler, James Endell, 1789–1851

C88a Indices Attici: or, a guide to the quantity of the Greek penultima, chiefly with references to Attic writers. [Anon.] Oxford, London: Printed by W. Baxter for J. Parker and G. and W. B. Whittaker, 1824.

xxxiii (1), 70 pp.

N's transcription of a letter from J. E. Tyler, July 5, 1824, at B.O.(B.12.1.): "Upon examining our *book* [[N.B.—the Indices Attici]] I am more and more pleased with the design and the execution." In N's Chronological Notes, his entry: "July 29. 1824 Worked at 'Indices Attici' with Tyler [which was published]."

D

Posthumous Publications
of John Henry Newman

Note: The following works have been arranged alphabetically by titles.

D1 Addresses to Cardinal Newman with his replies etc. 1879–81. Edited by the Rev. W. P. Neville. New York, London, and Bombay: Longmans, Green, and Co., 1905.

xxiii, 325 pp.

D2 The argument from conscience to the existence of God according to J. H. Newman. By Adrian J. Boekraad and Henry Tristram of the Oratory. Louvain: Editions Nauwelaerts, 1961.

205 pp.

Text of N's paper on the proof of theism.

D3 Cardinal Newman's doctrine of holy scripture according to his published works and previously unedited manuscripts. By Jaak Seynaeve. Louvain: Publications Universitaires de Louvain; Oxford: Basil Blackwell; Tielt: Uitgeverij Lanno, 1953.

408, 160 pp.

See John Henry Newman, *On the inspiration of scripture* (London, 1967), p. 19n.

D4 Catholic sermons of Cardinal Newman published, for the first time, from the Cardinal's autograph manuscripts. Edited at the Birmingham Oratory. London: Burns & Oates, 1957.

133 pp.

Same as **D6**.

D5 Correspondence of John Henry Newman with John Keble and others . . . 1839–1845. Edited at the Birmingham Oratory. London: Longmans, Green, and Co., 1917.

viii, 413 pp.

D6 Faith and prejudice and other unpublished sermons of Cardinal Newman. Edited by the Birmingham Oratory. [Introduction signed: C. Stephen Dessain.] New York: Sheed and Ward, 1956.

128 pp.

Same as **D4**.

D7 John Henry Newman: Autobiographical writings. Edited with introduction by Henry Tristram of the Oratory. London and New York: Sheed and Ward, 1956.

xi, 338 pp.

The same work was published in the United States in 1957.

D8 "John Henry Newman on Latin prose style: a critical edition of his *Hints on Latin composition.*" Vincent Ferrer Blehl, S.J. *Classical Folia*, XV (1961), 1-12. Text on pp. 5-10.

D9 The letters and diaries of John Henry Newman. Edited at the Birmingham Oratory with notes and an introduction by Charles Stephen Dessain of the same Oratory. Vincent Ferrer Blehl, S.J., co-editor of vols. XIV and XV; Edward E. Kelly, co-editor of vol. XXI; Thomas Gornall, S.J., co-editor of vols. XXIII–XXXI. Vols. XI–XXII: London, etc.: Thomas Nelson and Sons Ltd., 1961–72. Vols. XXIII–XXXI: Oxford: Clarendon Press, 1973–77.

Vols. I–X remain to be published.

D10 Meditations and devotions of the late Cardinal Newman. London and New York: Longmans, Green, and Co., 1893.

xvi (2), 438 (1) pp.

Reprinted in 1894, 1903, 1907, 1914, 1923, 1932, 1954, 1960.

D11 My campaign in Ireland. Part I. Catholic University reports and other papers by Cardinal Newman of the Oratory. [Advertisement signed: Wm. P. Neville.] Printed for private circulation only by A. King & Co. printers to the University of Aberdeen, 1896.

lxxxvi, 447, 28 pp.

D12 "The Newman-Perrone paper on development." Rev. T. Lynch. *Gregorianum*, XVI (1935), 402-47. Roma: Pontifica Università Gregoriana.

D13 Newman the Oratorian. His unpublished Oratory papers. Edited with an introductory study on the continuity between his Anglican and his Catholic ministry by Placid Murray, O.S.B., D.D., Monk of Glenstal. Dublin: Gill and Macmillan Ltd., 1969.
  xxv, 500 pp. Text: pp. 149ff.

D14 The philosophical notebook of John Henry Newman. Edited at the Birmingham Oratory by Edward Sillem and revised by A. J. Boekraad. Vol. II: The Text. Louvain: Nauwelaerts Publishing House, 1970.
  218 pp.
    Vol. I is a general introduction to the study of N's philosophy by Edward J. Sillem.

D15 Sayings of Cardinal Newman. London: Burns & Oates, Ltd.; New York: Catholic Publication Society Co., 1890.
  1-[iii], 76 pp.
    Newspaper gleanings. A collection of speeches and sermons delivered by N during his life as a Catholic. Some of these are only reports of speeches.

D16 Sermon notes of John Henry Cardinal Newman, 1849-1878. Edited by Fathers of the Birmingham Oratory with portrait. London, New York, Bombay, and Calcutta: Longmans, Green, and Co., 1913.
  xxiii, 344 pp.

D17 Sermon notes of John Henry Cardinal Newman, 1849-1878. Edited by Fathers of the Birmingham Oratory, etc. Second edition. London, etc.: Longmans, Green, and Co., 1914.
  xxiii, 347 pp.

D18 The theological papers of John Henry Newman on faith and certainty partly prepared for publication by Hugo M. de Achaval, S.J., selected and edited by J. Derek Holmes with a note of introduction by Charles Stephen Dessain. Oxford: Clarendon Press, 1976.
  xv, 170 pp.

D19 "An unpublished paper by Cardinal Newman on the development of doctrine." C. Stephen Dessain. *Journal of*

Theological Studies, n.s., IX, pt. 2 (1958), 329-35.
This same paper was also published by Hugo Achaval in *Gregorianum*, XXXIX, no. 3 (1958), 589-96.

General Index

Index of Titles and First Lines of Poems

General Index

References in this index are to item numbers in the catalogue. Initial definite and indefinite articles in titles are dropped in alphabetization. Titles and first lines of poems are placed in a separate index.

Discourses on university education, A17a

Discussions and arguments on various subjects, A18a-h

Dissertatiunculae quaedam critico-theologicae, A19a

"Dissertatiunculae quatuor critico-theologicae," A90a-d

Dr. John Henry Newman's reply to Mr. Gladstone's pamphlet, A20a

"Dr. Wiseman's *Lectures on the Catholic Church,*" B2d

"Downfall and refuge of ancient civilization," B6n

"Dream of Gerontius," B12a

Dream of Gerontius, A21a-l

Dublin Review, B10

"Duncan's Travels in North America," B4a

"Duties of the Church towards philosophy," A17a

"Ecce homo," B12c

Ecclesiastical history of M. L'Abbé Fleury, C17a, C18a, C19a

Echoes from the Oratory, A22a, A22b

"Ecole des Hautes Etudes at Paris," B6v

Education, C8

"Education movement in Ireland," B16i

"Elementary studies," A35a

"Elliott's *Travels,*" B21

Elucidations of Dr. Hampden's theological statements, A23a

Encyclopaedia metropolitana, C9a,b,c

"Entrance examination a trial of accuracy," B6e

Episcopal Church apostolical, C58a

Essay in aid of a grammar of assent, A24a-m

Essay on the development of Christian doctrine, A25a-j

Essay on the miracles recorded in the ecclesiastical history of the early ages, A26a

Essays critical and historical, A27a-k

Essays on controversial points variously illustrated, A28a

Eunuchus, C50a-d

"Examination at entrance," B6b

"Examination for the East India civil appointments," B6tt

"*Exeter Hall,*" B2i

"External difficulties of the Canon and the Catholic Creed, compared," C81a

"Faith and obedience," A80a

Faith and prejudice and other unpublished sermons of Cardinal Newman, D6

"Fall of La Mennais," A27a

"Family of St. Richard the Saxon," C31a

Fathers of the Church, C10

Fifteen sermons preached before the University of Oxford, A29a-f

Five letters on Church reform addressed to the "Record," A30a

Fleury, Claude, C17a, C18a, C19a

"Form of admission of a lay brother," A76a

"Form of admission of a novice," A76a

"Form of admission of a Triennial Father," A76a

"Form of infidelity of the day," A35a

"Forms of private prayer," A80a

Froude, Richard Hurrell, C20-21

"Gainsaying of Korah," A80a

"Gazette," B6ss

"General answer to Mr. Kingsley," A1a

"General knowledge viewed as one philosophy," A17a

"*Geraldine—A tale of conscience,*" B2g

Godly meditations upon the most

Index of Titles and First Lines of Poems

In listing titles of poems initial definite and indefinite articles have been omitted. They have been retained in listing first lines of poems. It should be noted that many poems in the "Lyra apostolica," British Magazine, have no title.